EXPOSING THE ABUSIVE FEMALE

D1601369

Kimberly C. Taylor, M.S.

Table of Contents

Preface

The abusive women project was created to take an honest and candid look at what is happening in relationships and how men are being abused by women in their lives. As a counselor and director of an agency who deals with intimate partner abuse, I have worked extensively with women who were victims of abuse. I have seen the devastation abuse has caused in their lives. Their abuse was significant at the hands of the men in their life.

But I questioned why I was not seeing many men coming in for counseling. I begin to ask, "Where are the men? I began discussing this with my friends and colleagues and that is when I began to hear the stories of men who had in fact been abused at the hands of their wives and girlfriends. They began to say, "I am one of those men, my wife abused me." As I started to tell one story, more became comfortable and they too told their story.

I knew that males who had experienced abuse were out there because I had been doing anger management and batterer's treatment groups for women and men for years. I knew that these men existed but I just didn't know if they would want to tell their story.

I began asking around and quickly found many who would tell their story. Once after doing an interview on TV I had a man come up to me who was cleaning the lobby at the TV station and tell me that he himself had been a victim of intimate partner abuse. With tears in his eyes, he said he was so glad someone was finally talking about the other side of domestic violence. I found as I talked about it that men everywhere started talking about what happened to them. It was as if it became okay to talk about the abuse they had experienced because others had been through it too.

I have since spoken to many men from every walk of life. Many successful, powerful, masculine men who tell the story of the shame they experienced at the hands of the female in their life. The abuse I am talking about includes verbal, emotional, financial, legal and physical. The men I have interviewed are considered very masculine and successful, yet had women who were very abusive. For many, they were raised to not hit a woman and they relied on the strong values of providing for their families and trying to maintain happiness in the home."

The goal of my project is to help people, both men and women, to look at the issue of abuse against men. The book contains stories of men who have been abused by their girlfriends/wives and of women who have been abusive. I go into the psychology of the abuse and my views on abuse against men based on my interviews and interaction with men who have been abused. I hope the project provides a balanced view to the issue of abuse and what is happening with men. This book gives their story and shows that they are from all walks of life and have an important message to tell the world and that message is that abuse is wrong no matter who it is against. Biases must be removed so we can accurately address the issue and most importantly, stop abuse against men, women and children in all its forms.

Dedication

This book is dedicated to every man who has wished they could tell someone that they were being abused by the female in their life.

This book is for every friend or family member who has seen their son, friend or brother being abused by their girlfriend or wife and didn't know what to do.

This book is dedicated to those who want to educate themselves about abuse against men.

This book is also dedicated to my mother Genevieve Fillmore. She has been a huge support in seeing the book get finished. Without her faith it would have been hard to finish the book.

This book is dedicated to my dear nana Helen Wilcox. She was my light and always believed in me beyond any belief in myself. Nana taught me to be fearless and live an adventurous life as it is much more interesting then not taking risks.

This book is dedicated to my grandfather Lewis Wilcox. He was a retired Air Force Colonel. He was a humble special man who had some heroic moments in his life.

This book is dedicated to my son, Chad Taylor, his amazing intuition, love and strength mean the world to me. His prayers for me have kept me strong through the hard times and given me hope in the outcome of this book changing lives.

This book is dedicated to Gina Graham. We have worked together for over 14 years in the field of domestic abuse and she is one of my most trusted friends.

This book is dedicated to my best friend Janet Du Bois May. We have been there for each other all these years through both good and bad times. I am grateful for having her in my life. She is a movie producer and I am proud of her.

I dedicate this book to Ollie, our white Labrador retriever who has been my companion during many late nights on the computer writing. He would climb on the couch next to me and just keep me warm or sit down by my feet as I typed away.

This book is dedicated to Scott Mac Fadden. He is an amazing man. I wouldn't have finished the project without his support and encouragement. We are blessed with each other and our great relationship.

This book is dedicated to my sister Jessica and brother Aaron who I love and am thankful for having in my life.

This book is also dedicated to Dr. John and Donna Mac Fadden, my second family. They are two of the most special and amazing people I have had in my life the last couple years.

Finally, this book is dedicated to everyone who helped me along the way with validating the topic and letting me know it was a project well worth the effort.

Most importantly, the book is dedicated to the men who told me their stories and poured their hearts out as they expressed the shame at the abuse and pain they suffered at the hands of their girlfriends and wives. They told their story so that other men in the same situation could see they are not alone and receive the courage to get help.

CHAPTER 1
History of Abuse

One may ask why a book about the exposure of the abusive female be written. The truth is there is a perceived "veil of immunity" that women have been able to exist within when it comes to abuse against men. Men have been left out with regard to abuse and being taken seriously as victims of intimate partner abuse (IPA) in today's society. Unfortunately, much of the history has focused only on the female victim leaving the male victim completely out with no validation.

Did you know that, in the United States, a man is abused by his female partner every 37 seconds? If you said "no," then you aren't alone. Thousands of men each year are victimized by IPA and either ignored or shunned in their fight for justice; the abuse they've suffered somehow deemed invalid or unreal.

History

Prior to the 1960s, what happened between a man and a woman in the privacy of their own home was considered to be a personal matter and off-limits to the police. Not until the early days of the Feminist Movement did we begin to talk about IPA on a national level. However, due to the nature of the movement, the focus was on the female victim and not the male. As a result, women were firmly established as the victims of intimate partner violence (IPV) with men identified as their perpetrators.

The Sixties

It first became widely unacceptable for a man to abuse his wife in the late 1960s. It was tough getting through that tumultuous decade for several reasons, but great changes were implemented, and women began receiving social support and access to services for the IPA they experienced.

According to the New York Department of Social Services, it wasn't until 1966 when "beatings" were officially acknowledged as "cruel and inhumane treatment" and became grounds for divorce. However, the plaintiff still had to establish that "a sufficient number of beatings had taken place," for a divorce to be allowed by the court.

In 1969, California helped lead the nation away from that by adopting a no-fault divorce law in which either partner could obtain a divorce, with the grounds for divorce no longer scrutinized by the court.

The Seventies

In 1974, the first women's shelter was opened, providing a safe haven and setting a new standard for the assistance provided for abused women. Hundreds of shelters for women would then be opened throughout the country in addition to the establishment of hundreds of intimate partner violence programs for women.

As these groundbreaking changes were occurring, it was not uncommon for a police officer at the scene of a domestic dispute to question both partners, only to tell the man to "go cool off and come back later." This was an early solution that continued to leave many victims still in harm's way.

Modern Day

It was not until the 1990s that the law enforcement community began to realize the true importance of intimate partner violence. Protocols and procedures were created for more effective interventions at the scene, which now included arresting the abuser. The police now also had the authority to issue an Emergency Protection Order (a restraining order that goes into effect immediately), making it illegal for the abuser to return to the residence or to approach or contact the victim.

Today, the police, the legal system, advocacy agencies, and crisis intervention groups have a much greater understanding of IPA and work together to provide the necessary intervention and assistance.

Solving the IPA Problem

The Feminist Movement in the United States will always be credited with recognizing the paramount problem of IPA in the homes of millions of families and setting into place a foundation for higher standards of conduct, personal freedom, and safety in relationships. The laws that protect us to this day would not be in place were it not for the women on the front lines who bravely encouraged battered women to speak out about what was happening to them. As a result, thousands of women continue to be saved from their abusive boyfriends and husbands.

These efforts have laid the groundwork for the next great battle: to reduce and eliminate all intimate partner violence against anyone who has experienced it, regardless of gender.

A Human Issue

At our heart we are a compassionate society, and we must speak out against abuse toward another human being in *any* form. We cannot tolerate it against women, men, or children. In order to effectively combat IPA, we must first think of it as a *human* issue and not a gender issue.

Though there may be aspects of gender involved in the case-by-case intervention and treatment of IPA, viewing it as merely a male or female issue fails to address the problem in its entirety. Both men and women are victims of abuse, emotional and physical. Both men and women are perpetrators of abuse as well. This must be recognized and openly discussed as a human issue, a relationship issue, and certainly a family issue, but not a gender issue at its core.

The "Veil of Immunity"

Approaching the problem of IPA as a gender issue only has proven to be one-sided and misleading, leaving many male abuse victims unacknowledged and unassisted in their attempts to deal with this very serious problem.

The Feminist Movement looked at male dominance and inequality in power for much of the abuse women experienced. These reasons did and do exist and should not be minimized, as they are issues relative to why females are abused. However, female-on-male abuse sometimes goes overlooked because women have a perceived "veil of immunity" in the event of IPA. Society's long-standing position of viewing women as the "weaker vessel," aside from being a false generalization, can be dangerous and should not be overlooked.

A Comprehensive Solution

To deal with IPA effectively in our communities, *all* victims of either gender must be advocated for. Likewise, abusers of either gender must be held accountable for their actions and provided the opportunity to change through effective treatment methods. Furthermore, the children of abusive relationships need help overcoming the damaging effects of their experiences, regardless of which parent is the abuser and which parent is being abused; the children of abused men cannot be left unassisted just because the idea of an abused man is too difficult for society to accept.

Conclusion

Though strides have been made, there is a great deal more to do in order to take the efforts of the Feminist Movement to the next level, which is to hold accountable the abuser no matter what the gender.

The bottom line is that, regardless of the reasons for abuse, abuse should not be tolerated for any gender. The "veil of immunity" must be torn down, and we must instead seek truth in how we view and handle human relationships.

CHAPTER 2
The Real Deal

Once I began to look at the issue of male victims of intimate partner violence, I began to question how prevalent of a problem male IPV was. What were the true statistics depicting how many men are actually being abused by their female partners?

The Evolution of a Perspective

We know that violence against women was gaining national attention in the 1970's. Researchers at that time began to question what the causes of abuse were in the home. Much of what they found led them to believe that there was a "gender inequality" directly linked to the abuse women were experiencing. The question at that time became, "Why are men so controlling and domineering toward women that they would resort to violence to keep women in a lesser position?"

The Feminist movement stated that it was the result of our Patriarchal society. The belief that with women in a lesser position men were bound to dominate and dominate to the extent of serious violence against women. There has been truth to this statement and their theory cannot be discounted. However, the issue is so much more complex when we discuss violence and abuse within relationships. What makes up each individual needs to be considered when it comes to abuse in relationships. Furthermore, as time has evolved and society along with it, women have made strides toward equality. It is important that we begin to look at the current research results and provide implementation strategies that will address the current research results and help clients in the most effective way.

What the Data Says

Dr. Murray Straus, Dr. Richard Gelles, and Dr. Suzanne Steinmetz were some of the first researchers to clinically examine the issue of family violence. Their efforts would provide tangible proof of violence against women in marriage and shed light on the dysfunctional dynamics of violent, domineering men. The results of the National Family Violence Study, a seven-year study of American families, revealed several surprising facts:

1) Women and men abused their spouses at *near equal* rates. That is, among families with histories of

violence (16% on average, nationally), when only one spouse was violent, the wife was the violent partner about half of the time.

2)In the majority of violent families, *both husband and wife* engaged in violent behavior toward each other. This was called "Mutual Violence."

Given our historical perception of the issue, the researchers did not expect to find gender equality among abusers. This could create an uncertainty in the women's movement and the beliefs it was propagating about men being the primary abusers.

The picture that is emerging from this research and others is that mutual violence exists in many of these homes and we have to restructure our interventions to address this fact. They found that among the 16% of families that reported violence, 49% were mutually violent, 24% had a violent wife, and only 27% of the time, the husband was the sole violent partner, (Straus, Gelles & Steinmetz, 1980).

Why?

I have found in my work with men and women that a sense of being personally out of control is at the core of abusive behavior. There exists a sense of entitlement by both the men and women who choose to use physical violence against their partner.

A Criminal Matter

One reason that intimate partner violence towards men is underestimated is that men are less likely to view the IPV against them as a crime, let alone report it to police. They typically think despite being violently assaulted that it is something they can handle because "after all, she is just a woman." In a 1985 survey, less than 1% of men who had been assaulted by their wives had called the police (Stet &Straus, 1992). In that same survey, men assaulted by their wives were less likely to hit back than were women assaulted by their husbands.

A Cry for Help

Men were also far less likely to call a friend or relative for help, with only 2% doing so. Societal norms for men seem to discourage reaching out for help in that situation (Goldberg, 1979). Considering that stigma, it is no wonder that men are also far less likely to receive a protection order from their female partner (Russell 2012). This supports the claim that male victimization is not taken as seriously in the courts, as these men were not seen as requiring protection at the same rate as women.

Proper Training for Proper Treatment

Police and the criminal justice system are steeped in the gender paradigm as it is part of the training given to new officers and officials. It is important for this training to include dynamics of mutual abuse and female perpetration of abuse against males. This is the only way to create a level playing field for those seeking help.

How the Numbers Lie

Legal Studies

A crime study conducted by the Department of Justice will measure the incidence of abuse when law enforcement and legal action come into play. This is important research, but it does have some limitations. By nature, it excludes all incidents of IPV that are not reported to police. This is exacerbated by the inherent fear men have that, if they call the police about a domestic disturbance, they may end up getting arrested and going to jail.

Additionally, there are many forms of abuse that are not illegal. Specifically, verbal and emotional abuse and certain types of threats are not punishable by law. Therefore, though crime study research is a vital and valid resource, it does not capture the full continuum of abusive behavior in relationships for men or women.

Shelter Studies

Shelter studies measure abuse only among victims whose circumstances have become extreme enough to require the safety of a shelter. The information gained from these self-report interviews has its place among the research, but it does not represent the average woman dealing with lower levels of violence from their partner.

Furthermore, we don't have comparative studies to draw from regarding men in shelters because there haven't been any shelters for men. That makes this method limited in its scope. Also, many shelter studies don't ask the women about any violent behavior they might have inflicted on their partner. Focusing only on the violence they endured is a significant oversight that further limits the veracity of these studies. Studies that have asked this question of victimized women have most often found mutual violence by both partners (Straus et. al., 1980).

CPS Reports

Much like shelter studies, studies conducted through Child Protective Services only report statistics within families whose dynamics are severe enough to warrant CPS involvement. Again, there is much to be gained by these studies. However, families whose dysfunction is less severe (as well as severe cases that are not reported for child abuse or neglect) will not be reflected in the results.

So, What Does Work?

Family violence studies examine a cross-section of families and relationships, measuring violent and non-violent relationships side by side. This research method provides a unique view into relationships and the nature of conflict. The scope of this type of research is broad, with a wide range of questions asked of both partners equally. Consequently, there are fewer assumptions made at the outset and fewer limitations as a result. This method appears to have a great deal to offer to the body of research on the subject.

To sum it up, the rates of abuse will vary, and this is by design. Depending on the people participating in the study and which questions are being asked, there can be very different results.

However, as long as we pay attention to where the results came from and how they were obtained, we can make sense of the differences that are inevitable and watch for biases and assumptions that may cloud the true results and interfere with the intervention services designed to help victims of abuse.

Conclusion

There are some who fear the implications of any research that sheds light on the abusive nature of some women. However, to look away from the overwhelming evidence, obtained again and again over three decades of research, illustrates a lack of courage behind the conviction. It discredits the abuse advocacy movement to allow such a dangerous bias to exist. To ignore men as victims of abuse for fear of what it may mean for women's advocacy is to promote and support abuse.

CHAPTER 3:
Fairytale to Nightmare

When I sat down with Mike for him to tell his story, there was a look on his face of relief. He was ready. He wanted to get the truth out about what his experience was like. Mike was a very attractive man with wavy dark hair and piercing blue eyes that appeared to have a steel strength in them. I began by asking him how he had met and fell in love with the woman who would later become his very abusive wife.

He began by saying that he had first only seen a picture of her. A friend of his had gone to prep school with her, and thought she was beautiful and Mike's type. Mike said he immediately wanted to meet her. She was reportedly very smart and an extreme athlete. He said, "I knew I had to meet this woman and so I set out on making it happen." Mike had made a successful living on Wall Street and had the temperament and boldness to "play with the big boys." He got involved in a highly competitive industry and did very well for himself. His focus was on making a lot of money and becoming the best at what he did.

Some time had gone by when he finally met this girl. "I was drawn in by how attractive she was and foolishly thought it was love at first sight." He asked her out, but she initially turned him down because she was dating someone at the time. Eventually, she agreed to go out on a date with him. Her reluctance only made him more determined. Mike recalls that she was somewhat cold on that first date, but very smart and interesting. He later would say that had he paid attention to the behavior and not merely her looks on that initial meeting, things would have turned out different. Nevertheless, they seemed to have much in common and he wanted to pursue her. "She had to like me," he said. He wanted to forge a relationship with her. She finally began to respond to him, and they fell in love very quickly. Mike remembers it was a very passionate beginning to what he hoped would become a long and happy life together. He felt he had met the woman he could marry and have a family with.

Mike had waited until his thirties to get married because he only wanted to be married once. He wanted to make sure that whomever he married would be the right girl for him. His parents had divorced when he was in the sixth grade, and it had been extremely devastating for him. Out of all of his siblings, he was the closest one to his mom and dad. Mike took some time to talk about his father and the love he had for him. He talked about how his father had served as a Marine in World War II and later in the Merchant Marines, and had a very forceful presence about him. Yet his father was not a strict disciplinarian. He was a good man who wanted to provide for his family and do the best he could. Mike said he cherished the closeness he had with his father and always looked forward to the times he would return home from being at sea. Mike had been raised in a Catholic home with many siblings. His family believed in God, was involved with the church, and held family to be very important. Both parents were from small towns so they had a mid western upbringing. Because family and religion were always important to him, this only added to the confirmation this girl was for him when he found out she was also Catholic. "She loved the same kind of art as I did and we had many similar interests." According to Mike, she was very hard to get, and in some ways, he valued that because it did not come easy like many things had for him. He also got along well with her family. When he went to tell her father he was going to ask his daughter to marry him, her father said, "Does she know that yet?" When Mike said, "No," her father responded with, "Well, good luck." Mike sighed in frustration as he said he knew early on in the dating relationship he had a "tiger by the tail." Mike remembers one time his future mother-in-law said about her daughter: "When she is good she is very, very good, but when she is bad, she is horrid." The mother had told Mike about a time when the children were very young. The girl had written her four-year-old brother's name across the wall and watched him take a beating for it when they found it.

In retrospect, he believes, much of what probably drew him to her in the beginning began to show itself in the extreme by the difficult nature of her personality. He said the spirited girl he was drawn too became very demanding and cold. In fact, during the engagement period of thirteen months, he began to have second thoughts due to how nasty she had become. He recalled one memorable incident: After she had moved in with him, he was out of town on business, and when he returned home and walked into his house, all of his expensive art and décor that lined the walls throughout his house had been taken down and replaced with her art and all of her things.

He was stunned because she had always complimented him on how he decorated and said she loved his art, rugs, and antiques. Yet she still took all of his things out of his own home. "She acted as if it was not a big deal and brushed it off." He began to realize she did not pay attention to his needs, and it became all about planning a big society wedding. He had no part in the decision-making. Instead of coming to decisions together, she would do what she wanted with no regard of his input.

He said he asked his sister, a psychologist, about her behavior, and the sister said that it may be stress related to planning the large wedding. However, the sister did say that it could potentially become a huge issue. Mike was hesitant, but he moved forward with his plans. He kept thinking things would get better and change when she got through it. Nevertheless, things did not improve, and the demanding, selfish behavior continued over the whole engagement. On the wedding day, he was pacing in the parking lot thinking about not going through with the wedding. During his pacing, his sister came out to the parking lot and said she had overheard one of the bride's friends say, "Well, now you can get whatever you want," and she replied, "you have got that right." Mike felt his heart drop and he was certain he should not go through with it; he was feeling the sense of doom at that very moment that had accumulated over the engagement period. He felt desperate and asked his sister what he should do. Her reply, as the music was beginning to play in the church, was: "Pour Holy Water on her and run like hell."

Mike said he would think and ponder about the advice of his sister many times in years following the wedding. He said he would daydream of what might have happened had he not gone through with the marriage ceremony. "What would things have been like?" He said emphatically that he wished he had not overlooked those signs. He went on to describe the honeymoon, where in his opinion, the cruelty started with her saying very hurtful and nasty things that completely shocked him. He could not believe she could be so cruel on their honeymoon of all times. He felt these really hurtful comments were designed to injure him. It was not so much swearing or name calling, but trying to impede him or attribute some heinous meaning to his behavior. He said with a confused tone, "She would actually accuse me of the very behavior she was doing." At one point, she even said, "I hate you and wish I would have never married you." The period that should have been so enjoyable, celebrating their love and their new union as husband and wife, had been tainted.

Mike said that during the marriage, things continued to go south very quickly when she was pregnant with their first child. They would eventually have four children together, but things turned nasty quickly before any had even arrived. He felt he did not have a say in anything around the house. In his opinion, it was all about her and her pregnancy, and her friends and family. According to Mike, the experience became surreal; it was as though he was observing his own life as an outsider. At one point, he tried to talk to her about this and express his feelings. She would say he was being controlling and selfish. The arguments became more frequent with her throwing tantrums and slamming doors. At this point, she had begun to see a therapist, and he went with her to therapy. He said she later hired and fired seven marriage therapists over the course of the marriage. Mike recalled that his wife had said her parents had a very stormy marriage with frequent angry outburst, which could include anything from throwing televisions at each other to breaking plates and dishes. He said one night when she was very sad, she told him that as a child her father came home one day and said he was leaving and taking half the children with him. That night when she went to bed, she laid half way under the bed and half way out from under the bed. She had told Mike about her parent's turbulent marriage growing up, and said it had a significant impact on her and her view of relationships. During Mike's marriage, when they would go see a counselor to work on their marriage, his wife would fire the counselor and hire a new one if the focus shifted to altering her behavior. He complied seven times before he said he would not go anymore.

Mike really wanted to make his family work. The thought of being away from his children was too painful. He really wanted the dream that he thought she shared with him. He wanted their lives to be filled with love and true intimacy. Despite being successful and aggressive in business, it was not something he could translate into his relationship no matter how hard he tried. At one point, it even became physical, where she would slap and hit him, and back him up against a wall, screaming. These episodes were very frightening. "Clearly, I could have defended myself, but I knew it would lead to getting into trouble myself, possibly even arrested," he said. He said he would try to leave, and when he would push her aside to get around her, she would say,

"Ouch, you hit me!" He knew he would be in a worse situation if he responded physically to her, so he would choose to instead leave to cool down. He did this many times. He would actually ponder if she *was* crazy, due to her violent outbursts and many mood swings. "I felt so alone in my own life. One night, we had a huge party at our beautiful home to raise funds for a charity. There were all these people there enjoying themselves, and I looked around and felt isolated and alone in my own home. I thought to myself, I cannot do this anymore." He conveyed that he wanted to experience a real, loving relationship with someone who truly loved him in return. According to Mike, this was one of many moments where he would contemplate what he was doing in the marriage, how to make things work, or how to get out with the least amount of damage to himself and his children.

Mike talked about his faith and how being a Catholic also held him back from leaving the relationship. "I believed in staying together and making it work." He said they sought help through the church and went on a twelve-weekend retreat, where there was intense journal writing and long twelve-hour days. It became real to him during that time that the reality that she saw and that she embraced were not his reality. He was so disappointed that after all the intense work they had tried to do, there was not really any resolution. He said the only thing it proved was that, "he had a high tolerance for pain and they were very fertile." He had four children without trying very hard so that was the blessing that came despite the suffering.

Finally, after ten years of marriage, he decided to leave. The idea of the dream dying had become less painful than the reality of the marriage. He had tried all that he could, and he made the final decision to start his own life away from her. He remembered a time earlier when they had filed for divorce the first time. His daughter was five at the time, and he was heartbroken over being away from her and her brothers. One night, they were in the hot tub, and he tried to explain to her that he would not be around much. She said, "Daddy, are you and mommy getting a divorce?" As he responded, "Yes," she asked, "Do you love mommy?" He said, "Yes, I love your mommy very much; she gave me you." She nodded and said, "That is good. Does that mean you won't be fighting all the time?" He looked into his daughter's eyes and said, "Yes, that is exactly what that means." She patted him on the back and said, "Well, then that is good, daddy."

CHAPTER 4
Single Father Survivor

When Jeff and I first sat down to go over his story, he was not sure if what he had experienced was abuse. He believed she was "crazy" and he had endured a lot with her, but he was unclear how to even define the experience of being married to a woman who, as he described it, "would foam at the mouth when she was angry." He described the look in her eyes as "madness." He was a bit uncomfortable talking about this personal and intimate part of his life, yet he felt a sense of relief in sharing his story and in getting the validation that what he had gone through with her was abuse. Many men think it is all them and that they should just endure the abuse.

Dreams Dashed

Jeff grew up in a middle-class family to both biological parents. His mother was a teacher and his father a doctor. He attended good schools and did well academically and socially. He played football in high school. He had a funny sarcastic wit and a way with the women. Soon after graduation, Jeff was recruited to become a fighter pilot. He trained in Florida at the top of his class and was set to become one of the country's "Top Guns."

During a routine physical, the doctors discovered Jeff was color blind, and his dream of soaring through the air at mach speed came to an end. He fell into a mild depression and wondered what his options were for the future. He was very intelligent, so a career would not be an issue, but fulfilling his life-long dream was now impossible.

A New Hope

After a period of solitude, Jeff focused on a new career and began building a business in insurance sales. It was during this time that Jeff started going out with a beautiful woman he had met at the bookstore. He thought she was amazing, and they moved in together soon thereafter.

At first they could not get enough of each other's company. However, Jeff noticed she began to want to go on extravagant trips and spend money they didn't have. Jeff said she began to work for a doctor, and that she was always talking about him and his money and how nice he was.

Decline

Jeff felt they had a good relationship, and he wanted it to work. But they began to communicate less, with Jeff focusing on his job and not spending much time with his girlfriend. She would stay out late at night, and he began to feel very distant from her.

She eventually left for her physician employer. There was a coldness he felt that he wanted desperately to get rid of. He had spent a significant amount of time building a business and trying to make a good living. He had a big hole in his heart and went to work only to focus on making more money.

Jeff felt at a loss for what he had done to contribute to the end of his first long term relationship. He emerged wounded and confused about women. Unfortunately, he didn't take the time to analyze what had failed in that relationship before he once again approached the world of dating. He needed to look inward more at this time rather than cover up the pain. If he would of taken even a short time to look inward and see what his part was in the contribution to the end of the relationship he would have been better prepared for the world of dating.

Lisa

The next woman he would become serious with would turn out to be a very abusive woman. At first Lisa was very positive and fun to be around. He got a lot of physical attention he did not get from his previous girlfriend and became drawn into the relationship. She was not particularly striking in her looks, but it was nice for him to have that physicality. He felt safe with her because he thought she was very content with him.

Family Life

Lisa became pregnant early on in the relationship and they had a son. Jeff was very excited to be a father, and he wanted the boy to have both parents. He married Lisa and they began their life together.

At first, Lisa was a good mother. She was attentive to the baby and took good care of him. However, when he was about three months old, she began drinking at home during the day. She would call Jeff and demand he come home and take care of the baby. Many times he would leave work and come home to find her passed out while the baby played alone. He became very fearful for his son's life and his wife's health.

He brought in childcare to help with the baby, but Lisa would send them home and continue to drink around the baby. Jeff tried to get her help with her alcohol use, but she continued to deny she had a problem. She would have huge mood swings and go into rages for no apparent reason. He was able to get her to see a psychologist who diagnosed her as bipolar, but she would not take her medication and continued to act unstable. This carried over into every area of her life. He felt everything he tried didn't work when it came to getting her help.

Also of concern for Jeff was their intimacy and sex life. Lisa was very attentive to Jeff's needs when she was feeling good. However, about six months into the marriage, she became very non-sexual with him and began to cheat on him. He found out when a friend saw her with a man one evening and snapped a photo of them on his cell phone. Jeff was shocked. When Jeff confronted her, she became enraged and began to slap him. She kept calling him a liar and hitting him over and over. He didn't leave her because of his son.

Lisa also started to act out in public by doing embarrassing things in restaurants and stores. She would always complain about something and demand things from the waiters and clerks. If she didn't get her way in a store she would throw a fit. These public scenes could last for hours. This made Jeff very uncomfortable. He was raised with manners and it was particularly embarrassing to him.

It Gets Worse

The physical violence became more frequent. After the initial incident, it was about a month before her next violent outbreak. At first, if she wasn't getting her point across, she would take the remote control and smack it until it broke, or she would throw pillows at him, not necessarily things that would hurt. But it increasingly got worse until she was throwing candelabras at his head and things that would hit the wall and crash. It was only a year later that she began to hit with her hands and punch him with her fists. He knew he could defend himself, but he was shocked at her violence and hatred directed at him.

As time went on the violence escalated to about once a week with the serious violence occurring about once a month. She would come in drunk in the middle of the night and just start punching him and yelling at him. He continued to endure the violence because he did not want to lose his son. He was afraid she would win in a custody battle. About a year later, she quit drinking so much. However, the violence continued.

Most of the time, Jeff would go numb and just sit there, not saying much. They would sit in the dark, and she would go on and on degrading him for hours.

The Fear of Seeking Help

He threatened to call the police a few times after she had hit him, but he was nervous about being blamed for the incident. She was very dramatic, and he had no idea what would happen once the police arrived. Would it be him instead of her to go to jail? "Sometimes we would get in a fight, and she would say I hit her, and that would scare me," he confessed. "She would block doors, and I would try to move her, and she would yell that I was abusing her. She was completely out of control. I eventually began to say really mean things back to her and found that we were verbally abusive toward each other at that point, and I did not want to become like her."

Jeff actually thought much of it was his fault at first and went to see a therapist to improve his communication skills. He felt depressed that she was always yelling at him and name calling and fighting. He would have sex with her occasionally, but even then he felt totally disconnected and angry. It got to where the thought of her touching him made him sick, and he did not want any intimacy with her at all.

He originally did not know how to express feelings, and if he had resentment, he would just keep it in. He felt responsible for her and concerned she would go off the deep end or commit suicide.

Escape

He began spending time alone in a special park he would go to. In these times of meditation, he realized he did not want to take the blame for all of her psychotic behavior and be embarrassed every time they went to dinner together or to a friend's house to visit. He did not want to spend the rest of his life with her. In fact, he did not want to spend another moment with her. There was a moment of crystal clear revelation that this woman was never going to change, and he absolutely did not want to be a part of her life anymore. In order to ever be happy, he would have to get out, and the sooner the better.

There was one very scary event that happened when she became distraught. "She was always depressed," he said. "One day she was in one of these states, and she kept calling my work complaining about our son, slurring her words and mumbling about hating her life."

Jeff was upset because he had to leave work, but when he got home, she had thrown every piece of glass in the house at the wall, shattering them into a million pieces. The baby was crawling around the outside of the glass. Jeff gasped and grabbed him. She yelled and came charging at him, hitting him with both fists, barely missing the baby's head. "I hate you, I hate you, I hate you," was all she kept repeating. She had a glazed, angry look in her eyes he had never seen.

At that moment he knew he couldn't wait to get out. He called her mother to come over to get her, and he walked out of the house with the baby, Lisa screaming and running behind him, throwing things at their backs.

A few days later, Jeff went to see a divorce lawyer who said to him, "Look, I understand. I went through something similar. Do you want to get out?"

Jeff looked across the table and thought for a moment, then said, "Yes, I do want to get this divorce started right away."

He got a storage unit and began putting away items that he would need when he moved out. He went to look at apartments and found one he really liked. His spirits were getting higher, and he found himself feeling happier and stronger as he began to picture his new life without the constant abuse he had endured for ten years.

Living with PTSD

The anxiety Jeff suffered is not unusual for one who has Post Traumatic Stress Disorder. Many women and men who experience domestic violence then suffer from PTSD. Symptoms include hyper-arousal, panic, rapid heartbeat, and anxiety. They can be triggered by noises or situations that remind them of the traumatic event.

Although Jeff was physically bigger than this woman, he had endured so much abuse that he was experiencing some of these symptoms and feeling severe anxiety at the thought of running into her. He could have called the cops or applied for a restraining order, but he felt he may not get it, and he did not want to run the chance of having to see her at all ever again. He had no idea what she was capable of.

After weeks went by, he felt calmer and more relaxed. He began to visualize his life ahead of him, even though he was not sure how it all would go. He wanted to do things he had not done in a very long time, like visit friends, and spend time doing things he used to love to do. He had become hopeful for a change and believed he could have a better life.

He had a divorce attorney, but he figured she would get a lot of money since he had a good job and she had not been working. The next couple of years were very stressful dealing with the divorce, but it was worth every moment. Jeff had to fight for custody of his son, but he was awarded full custody with Lisa having supervised visitation, which was lifted to unsupervised visitation after she completed drug and alcohol counseling and anger management.

Conclusion

Being a single father has been a struggle for Jeff, but he said, "I wouldn't change getting out for anything. If I would have stayed, there is no telling what could have happened, and I want to be there for my son."

He needed to go to therapy to address his fears of new relationships, and as of the writing of this book, had not yet done so. He still has great fear of relationships and of women. He still has hopes and dreams that someday he wishes to fulfill, but his experience left him deeply scarred. The reminder of his experience continue to haunt him as he has sought to move forward with relationships.

It is unfortunate that one abusive woman could so change a man's perspective and faith in love. My hope is that someday he will reach a place where he can risk again and be vulnerable in a relationship with a loving and caring woman. He deserves a great relationship.

CHAPTER FIVE

HE KNEW HE WAS A GONER

When I met Matthew I was very surprised to learn he had experienced abuse at the hands of his wife. He was a professional baseball player with a larger-than-life personality, a contagious laugh, and a brilliant smile. He has transformed a career in professional baseball into a successful business. Matthew is very engaging with a passion and understanding of current events and politics. He loves his children and has always made it a top priority to be actively involved in their daily lives. He was a devoted husband and a caring father throughout his 17 years of marriage. The big issue for Matthew was that his marriage had no passion and no intimacy left to speak of. As this was a very important relational component for Matthew, he knew his marriage would not last. They eventually divorced and remained close friends.

The void that was left in Matthew's life was a strong drive for an intimate and passionate relationship. He was open and searching for some excitement. That is when Rachel walked into his life. At first she seemed like a beautiful person. Rachel was a fun girl whom Matthew met through a mutual friend. What added to his initial attraction was that she had a graduate degree and a business of her own. She appeared to have it together.

They quickly fell into the "passionate and all-consuming fling," Mathew longed for. Matthew and Rachel began a long-distance relationship between the West Coast to the Mid-West, spending most of their weekends together. Matthew only had the opportunity to see her at her best. The long-distance arrangement lasted quite some time, which is a warning sign for relationships because one never really sees the person when they are at their worst. It is the constant party and good behavior. But after two and half years of excitement and weekend fun they moved in together. Rachel moved her pre-teen daughter and herself to Matthew's Orange County California home.

In the initial couple months the honeymoon continued. They had been living together a couple months when Matthew and Rachel bought a house together in an upscale neighborhood. Within a short time, the veil of deceit would lift and Matthew would see a side of her he did not know existed. He would be floored by the mean spirited and abusive nature that made itself evident after a short time.

Rachel became all about gaining the attention of other men. She would dress extremely provocatively to go to dinner and anywhere else they would go together. She became unresponsive to Matthew's attention because it became not enough for her; she wanted lots of male attention and did not care what it took to get it. Matthew was taken aback by her tactics to get attention and flirt obnoxiously with other men in front of him. Matthew chose to ignore it.

Over the next six months he went about intently building his business. They had been living a very comfortable life in their upscale home when Rachel decided to inform Matthew that things are going too fast for her. Her idea to save the relationship is for them to live separately for a while and still see each other exclusively, like a normal dating relationship, which they had never had. Matthew wanted the relationship to work, so he moved out of the home they bought together thinking they would work on the relationship. Matthew did not feel good about this arrangement and time would reveal her true intentions. Within several weeks of him moving out,

Rachel began dating other men. In fact, she began dating many men.

Matthew and Rachel continued to see each other, as he was not aware of her dating other men at the time. He began to notice some things about Rachel's behavior that were concerning. Rachel would loudly accuse him of looking at other women when they went out. She made a scene in a grocery store when she thought he was staring at the cashier. She threw the receipts at his face in the store and stormed out. It was here that Rachel began to project onto Matthew the exact behavior she was guilty of: cheating on their supposed exclusive commitment. She knew she was wrong, but convinced herself it was his fault; this resulted in her punishing him by picking a fight and causing a public scene. Her behavior was blatant and many of her friends were aware of her indiscretions. She was not doing much to hide her dating life.

On one occasion Rachel was extremely anxious and ranting around the house saying very demeaning things to Matthew that were completely out of the blue. He could see her escalating to a full rage and he wanted to try and get her to calm down. He followed her and as she stood in the doorway, asked her to talk about what was bothering her. She pulled back her arm and fully slapped him against his cheek. She had a ring on her finger and the cut on his face began to bleed. He asked her if she had gotten it out of her system. Instead of calming down, she became increasingly agitated and slapped him again. This time she didn't stop and continued to slap him again and again. Matthew held up his hand to avoid the continued slaps. As he sought to protect himself from the continued slaps, she began to say, "This is abuse, you hit me." She began to threaten to call the cops and to have him arrested for abuse.

Matthew was fearful but angry and told her to go ahead and call the police since he was the one standing there with blood dripping down his face. Rachel did not call the police but instead stormed out of the room continuing in her rage. This rage went on for five hours before she finally calmed down.

Matthew says to this day he doesn't recall any particular thing that set her off that day. He said it became very typical for her to be set off at the smallest thing.

For whatever reason, Rachel began to use violence on a regular basis toward Matthew to express her anger. She also began to accuse him of the very thing she was doing. Rachel's out of control behavior became evident on a regular basis with constant outbursts involving both hitting and yelling. Matthew would try and talk with her when she calmed down to ask her to get help and counseling to address her anger issues. However, Rachel would not even acknowledge her behavior and instead told him he needed counseling because he was controlling and drove her to act as she did. She would constantly yell at him and say, "You're so controlling, selfish, and angry! I hate you!" She would say demeaning things to him about how he wasn't a real man and she needed someone who could meet her needs. She would also say how horrible he was in bed and use verbal abuse to demean him sexually.

As her out of control behavior continued to come out, things went from horrible to unbearable and Matthew eventually told Rachel she had to move out. After much reluctance, she eventually moved back to the Midwest.

Matthew spent a lot of time trying to understand what had gone so wrong for them. He was wounded and felt a sense of guilt for the failure of the relationship. He deep down believed he could of made it better had he just done something different.

This is very common among men who are abused. They take responsibility for the abusive behavior that they see in their partner.

Despite it all, Matthew began to put his life back together and started attending a local church. He was doing well despite his lingering questions about the mysterious collapse of his relationship with Rachel. She had changed so dramatically from the woman he fell in love with. She seemed to blame him for her perpetual anger and discontentment. Nothing was ever enough for her, as she became less interested in Matthew and more interested in what he could do for her and give to her in a monetary way.

Several months after she had left, he was still putting the pieces of his life back together when the phone rang. It was her. She was very nice to him and asked in a very concerned tone how he was doing. She went on to say how she had done a lot of reflecting, and had realized that a lot of went wrong was because of her. She even said she had gone to a doctor and found out she was bi-polar. She said she had just begun taking medication and was "dramatically better." It seemed like a "miracle." She came across so nice and concerned, and most of all, wanted to see him and "start over." He was very hesitant but agreed to see her. He would reflect later that he should have trusted his instincts.

His girlfriend suffered a chemical imbalance and could not help but act the way she did. At least that was the explanation he was given by her. After several phone conversations, Rachel arrived on the doorstep with bags in hand. Matthew was not ready to see her but she just showed up on the doorstep uninvited. She pleaded with him for another try at making it work.

Matthew agreed and what he initially saw would blow him away. She appeared very attentive to him and not as flirtatious to men they were around. Her attitude was positive and she was open to new possibilities. Her approach to Matthew was loving and appreciative, not in the least bit argumentative or demanding.

One evening during her visit, Matthew showed Rachel a DVD he had been watching that tied his new belief in God to some of the goals he was working on personally and professionally. Rachel was so intrigued. She said this was exactly what she needed: God in her life and a deeper meaning to her existence. She said she wanted nothing more than reconciliation and God to be part of their lives now. The two grew close quickly. Rachel began to attend church with Matthew and talk all about God and what He was doing in her life. Things were moving forward but faster than Matthew had imagined.

Sudden, dramatic changes in a person following a complete disaster of a relationship may be the flip side of the same behavior. Real change takes sincere effort, inner healing and most of all, *time*. The test of time is the most important key to knowing what change is real and what is transient. Matthew should have allowed distance and time to test the relationship changes.

Medication can be a very important component for someone addressing a chemical imbalance they may be experiencing. However, there is a lot more to changing one's behavior than merely getting on psychotropic medication. In Matthew's situation, it appeared that Rachel had made a complete and total transformation and had become the woman of his dreams. This would prove to be a very false statement and a hope that would turn devastating. As the old adage goes, "If it seems too good to be true...perhaps it is too good to be true." As for the type of chemical imbalance, Matthew never thought to ask. What about the medication she was taking? He did not ask about that either until later on, after looking at the bottles and finding she was actually taking six different medications – all opiates. She was taking painkillers.

In a whirlwind Matthew and Rachel were married the same week she moved back to the West Coast. While they drove up the coast for a honeymoon on the beach, Rachel's emotionally abusive side came out. Rachel began to put him down about his performance sexually and pick apart his looks. She was distant and cold the first night of their honeymoon. The following day, Matthew asked her to join him for a glass of wine and to watch the sunset together. She got a disgusted look on her face and said, "Why would I want to do that?" She refused, and told him she was going to take a walk instead. When Matthew attempted to join her, Rachel snarled, "I don't want you to come with me. Do we have to spend every waking moment together?!" After she returned from her walk on the beach, Rachel told Matthew she had met a man on the beach who was "hitting on her." She was taunting him with comments about how she wished she had not married him, and how good-looking the guy was who had been hitting on her. She effectively shut the honeymoon down in the most demeaning way possible by stating she wished she was with the other man she had merely seen on the beach earlier that day.

When they returned home and began living life together, Rachel continued to say things to upset and belittle Matthew as the emotional abuse escalated. The "miracle" had become a nightmare. Comments such as, "You are so ridiculous," "You know I can't stand you," "You're getting old and going bald," and "I never should have married you. I should have married a rich man," are just a few of the unkind words Rachel dropped in passing.

One day, Rachel came home late into the evening from being gone all day and told Matthew she wanted to join the single's group at church. Matthew reminded her it would inappropriate to go to a single's group because she was married. Rachel laughed and told him to relax, saying that she only wanted to meet female friends and that the women's group was boring. Matthew was seeing that she was not the same woman who had originally been abusive to him: she was even worse in both emotional and physical abuse.

On another occasion, Rachel told Matthew she and her daughter were going to spend three weeks in Europe, and gave him the itinerary she had already booked with his money. Matthew was not invited. When Matthew suggested they make it a family trip for all of them, she told him he was cheap, controlling, and useless.

A short time later, when Matthew was in a rare, jovial mood, Rachel decided this was the perfect moment to tell him about all the other men she had sex with behind his back before they were married; yet she asserted she did not do anything wrong because they were not married yet. Her intention was to make Matthew feel horrible. This is abusive control at work on an emotional level. When things are said that hurt the other person intentionally they are being emotionally abusive.

As time went on, Rachel made a habit of physically attacking Matthew while he was driving the car. On many occasions, en route to church services, the grocery store, or anywhere at all, she would start slapping and hitting him. Matthew would turn the car around, leave Rachel at home, and go without her. Outbursts at home often involved the violent destruction of property as well. And then one night, while he slept she pounced on him and began her attack. After a disagreement earlier in the day about their choices for buying a new home, Rachel slept down the hall; as the clock reached 1:00 a.m., Matthew felt a stiff nudge on the shoulder. Rachel was standing over him saying, "I cannot take this anymore. I cannot take you. I hate you! I cannot stand you!" She started to cry and began hitting him in the face and chest with her fists. Matthew had been sound asleep and was caught off guard. As he realized she was beating him, he lifted his hands to block her blows. He leapt from the bed and yelled at her: "What the hell are you doing?" She ran down the hall into her daughter's room where she had been sleeping earlier. Matthew struggled to regain his composure. After considering his options, he headed down the hallway. As he entered the room Rachel said, "Get out!" making reference to her daughter's presence. Matthew began to yell at her, "You are crazy, and don't you ever hit me again... I have had enough of your abuse!"

He walked back down the hall and slammed the door behind him. This time he locked it. That night he prayed and asked God to help him.

The next morning, Rachel came into the bathroom to brush her teeth as though nothing ever happened. Matthew asked her if she had anything to say to him; Rachel smugly said, "No, what do you mean?" This time, Matthew was not about to let it go. "I want to talk to you about you attacking me in the middle of the night. You need help. You're abusive." Rachel looked over with a look of disdain on her face and replied, "Oh. Well, maybe I shouldn't have hit you," as she glided out of the room with ease.

Matthew decided to talk to someone about what was going on. He spoke with a friend who is a psychologist who warned him he may be in very serious physical danger living with her due to her frequent and violent outbursts. His friend was concerned about the ambush attacks that occurred at night when he was unaware and vulnerable physically. He felt she was unstable and possibly capable of killing him. Matthew decided to sleep in a separate room each night locking the door for his own protection.

Matthew made one last attempt to save the relationship by going to therapy, insisting he and Rachel needed to receive counseling. After several sessions, the counselor informed Matthew he felt there was no real chance for healthy change in the relationship because she was unwilling to look inward and accept responsibility for any of the problems they were dealing with. Rachel continuously blamed everything that went wrong on Matthew.

Matthew asked her to move out of the home, and she complied. She began to stop by regularly, as though this was just a rough patch in their relationship. Matthew found he was now facing a great deal of guilt for giving up on her and his

Christian vow to make it through tough times. They still owned a house together, which gave Rachel a reason to have contact with him, and she used that to get attention from him when she was feeling lonely and the other men she was seeing were unavailable.

Eventually Rachel moved back to the Mid-West once again but continued to telephone and email Matthew regularly. She had several ideas for reconciliation including staying married and flying in for sex here and there, and additional therapy that Matthew should get so he can resolve his issues that created their problems.

Matthew finally had the "moment of clarity" that people talk so frequently about with regard to life issues, and in that moment, he realized he wanted to stay away from this woman and get on with his life for good. There was no going back. There was no picking up the phone anymore. He deleted her from his phone, blocked her number, and did it with such determination and satisfaction because he knew it was the best decision he had ever made.

Once he made the decision to never go back, he met a beautiful woman at church. She was funny and engaging and had a kindness he had never known before. Despite her being very attractive, he was primarily drawn to her heart and her sense of herself, which came across in such an appealing way. She was unlike anyone he had dated before and he was very intrigued. They ended up dating for several years before getting married. When I spoke with him he said he believes he made the best choices for his life and he is very excited about the future with the loving woman he now has in his life.

CHAPTER 6
The Female Abuse Cycle

First of all, you cannot immediately spot her, unless of course she is hitting a man in front of you or verbally lashing him with her harsh words over dinner in your presence. Certainly, these are obvious clues. But you cannot assume anything based on economic status, religious affiliation, political party, body shape and size, public demeanor, looks, intelligence, or career status. There are women of all walks of life who present very well in public, but at home they can be just as abusive as their male counterparts.

Through my counseling with women who have an abusive anger language and the men who have experienced this abuse, I have begun to see a new cycle that exists when women are the identified abuser.

When domestic violence advocates typically thinks of the cycle of abuse, there are several stages the abuser goes through according to the "power and control wheel," that evolved out of many discussions with battered women through the

Domestic Abuse Intervention Project (DAIP) in Duluth Minnesota in 1980-1981. This begins with escalation to the explosive stage or outburst of violence phase, and then transitions to the cooling-down phase, and ultimately finishes with the honeymoon phase before the cycle is repeated. This has been illustrated and well known for quite some time as the standard cycle of abuse that has at its core the need for control by the abuser. Many incidences of abuse by men fall into this cycle. Some male abusers who become very violent continue in the abuse phase and do not enter the remorse phase or honeymoon phase. They maintain a level of violence and do not resort to any other phases.

Anecdotally, I have identified a different cycle among women in batterer's treatment groups and individual therapy. This cycle is characterized by methods of coercion and manipulation, that when not heeded, is followed by emotional and/or physical abuse. Once the explosion occurs and the woman has attacked the man verbally and/or physically, she retreats for a short time before justification and denial ensues. She will either become quiet and avoid contact for sometime, or she will act as though nothing ever happened and justify all bad behavior. Unlike with men, there is generally no period of insight where they will sometimes acknowledge their bad behavior

With many men, the honeymoon phase is characterized by the abusive partner being very remorseful for the abuse and saying things like, "I am sorry, I wish you hadn't pushed me to the point where I had to hit you," or "I love you and I promise I will never do it again." Sometimes this is accompanied by very nice behavior and gifts. It typically leaves the abuse victim stunned by the abuse and confused by the remorse. Yet, the abusive women I interviewed said this was not the case for them. When I asked them why they never felt remorse, I received differing opinions. Some said they thought no one would take their spouse seriously since they were women. Others said they believed their partners deserved it. They all had varying reasons, but the common component was they just did not feel remorseful. Most of them said they would just go on with "business as usual" and any confrontation would be met with great resistance and minimization.

Perhaps it is because society is less condemning and more dismissive of a woman who is abusive, resulting in less societal awareness and consequently more room for personal denial. It is also possible that the male is even less aware that they are being abused and may even take more responsibility due to the same lack of societal awareness. In short, the dynamic in the relationship may allow for this denial.

In a recent recent study noted (Gelles 2006), about fifty percent of men and women thought it was okay for a woman to hit a man. With these global attitudes, it is no wonder some women feel justified in slapping their partners. Some even said they knew they could not do too much damage because of their size; they therefore minimized their actions and denied it was abuse at all.

The men I interviewed said repeatedly that the women in their life never apologized for the abuse and never even acknowledged they were abusive. Surely, there are some women who do apologize and who do acknowledge this behavior and recognize that it is wrong. However, more often than not, they are not even admitting it exists. It seems the more we raise awareness that women do slap, hit, and abuse at rates almost equal to men, the more men and society will be likely to hold women equally accountable for their bad behavior, just as society does toward men who abuse. As research has demonstrated consistently, the majority of abuse within relationships is mutual combat, meaning both parties are abusive toward each other at almost equal rates (Straus, M.A., Gelles, R.J. & Steinmetz (2006) Kessler, R.C., Molnar, B.E. Feurer, I.D. & Applebaum, M. (2001).

Why should women get away with abusive behavior when men are not allowed to? Abuse is never okay, and it is very important for there to be accurate assessment of who is the abuser in the relationship. Law enforcement and the courts have a responsibility to make the most accurate determination regarding intimate partner violence to correctly assess the identity of the dominant aggressor.

In many studies, women are more significantly abused, yet they initiate the violence more often than men. According to the U.S. Department of Justice Intimate Partner Violence statistics, male victims were threatened with a weapon 22.9 percent, while females reported being threatened with a weapon 17.6 percent. Women reported the type of attacks at a greater percentage than men with the following forms: rape, sexual assault, attacked with firearms, attacked with knives, grabbed, held, and tripped. Men were also at a greater percentage for being hit by a thrown object.

It was also noted that females were more likely than males to seek treatment for their injuries. In the same study, the male victims said they did not report the incident primarily because it was a private or personal matter. They were also more likely to not report it in order to protect the offender.

I try to work with female abusers to help them take responsibility for their abusive behavior, just like we as a society have asked men to do for years. When I talk with these women candidly in group meetings and explore with them how they perceive their abusive behavior, they do feel remorseful when they are confronted with the truth. When they take a look at how their behavior has impacted their loved ones, they are often saddened and want to make a change in their lives. However, this mirror needs to be held up so they can see clearly how it has impacted those they love. Examining oneself candidly is no easy task, but it is freeing for them and allows them to recognize that they have control over how they act.

CHAPTER 7
Sugar and Spice is not Always Nice

I have seen many women make the necessary changes and turn their lives around. There are some factors that, when present in combination with one another, cause a woman to be at a greater risk for being abusive. Some of these risk factors include a fragmented past history, unresolved trauma with fear of intimacy, unrealistic expectations of their partner, risk-taking behavior, possessive control, jealous rages, extreme anger, and a history of mental disorders, such as Narcissistic Personality Disorder and Borderline Personality Disorder. The more risk factors a woman has from this list, the more likely she is to be abusive.

Past History
Does the woman in this man's life have a fragmented past history? Are there holes or gaps that are not adequately explained? The human psyche is good at protecting itself from painful done through

repression, even from our own conscious awareness of the trauma. Experiencing trauma on some level can be described as being part of the human experience. However, if someone has experienced a significant amount of trauma there will be residual effects that will carry over into their everyday life. According to Sciencedaily.com, in a recent study done by the Mayo Clinic, a history of child abuse among depressed inpatients was linked to an increase in suicide attempts, a greater prevalence of substance abuse, and a higher incidence of personality disorders. Sometimes this trauma becomes expressed through abusive behavior. At the very core of the behavior, you may find deep seated insecurity.

Some women who are exposed to intimate partner violence while growing up become either a victim or an abuser in their adult relationships. This is also true for men according to national statistics (Stith, 2006)

Many of the women I interviewed said that they did not have a father figure in their lives, and did not experience a healthy relationship with a man growing up. They felt a desperate need for male attention, yet simultaneously experienced a strong distrust of men and their motives. This paradox can become a hindrance in having a healthy interpersonal relationship with a man.

Our past is what brings us to the present with all the memories, experiences, challenges, and joys. It shapes us as we become adults. When people start relationships, they want to ask some candid and honest questions such as: what do they believe about relationships, trust, love, marriage, faithfulness, honesty, and vulnerability? Their views on these things are very important going into a relationship. They are who they are and it is very important for them to acknowledge that they will not and cannot change anyone, so they need to be willing to accept their partner just as they are. It is always said that women try to change the men in their lives. The truth is that we all, both men and women, have a desire to change things about someone else. Men want to change the women in their lives, as well. The truth is that a man cannot wipe away a woman's past, just like he cannot wipe away his own past; he can only go from where he is and move forward, and if she does not want to move forward and have a healthy relationship, it is time for change.

Unresolved Trauma with Fear of Intimacy

A person who has experienced abuse will typically have a fear of intimacy on some level. The level of resolution they have is important in determining the level of closeness and shared intimacy they acquire in a relationship, and the level their partner may experience. This is important to know as one begins a new relationship. One must really take to heart that it may be a long and winding road toward healing, and that this journey takes much patience and understanding. A person who has a tendency toward abusive behavior will also show a fear of intimacy

They might be very uncomfortable with intimate, caring, non-sexual attention; instead, their attention may remain very sexually focused and their desire to remain distant emotionally will show itself through this hyper-sexuality. This fear of intimacy can also be expressed by the neglect the man may feel emotionally when she refuses to connect with him on any deeper level. *It is important to not confuse sexual contact with emotional intimacy*. In order to protect herself, one woman said that by keeping a hard exterior, she thought she was keeping her partner in the relationship. The unfortunate reality is that they are generally pushing their partner away because their partner's emotional needs are not being met. I work with these women to embrace their vulnerability as strength and not a weakness. If a woman is not connecting on any real emotional level, she is either not really interested in the man in her life or has a fear of intimacy that is preventing this emotional connection. This does not mean she will be abusive; however, a man may feel very emotionally neglected in the relationship. Many times this fear of intimacy does carry over into sexual intimacy or lack thereof, and a woman who experiences this will make excuses for not having sexual contact. If this is the case, it is important to seek professional counseling to resolve any latent issues. It is important to not think that over time things will get better if nothing is resolved to any degree. The fear of intimacy is not easily overcome.

Many of the women who become abusive do not have many close relationships with other females in their lives. They are isolated from close, intimate friendships with women. They may want relationships with other women, but have had a hard time sustaining them. They have a distrust of other women and an inability to create honest, sharing, supportive friendships with females. As a result, they have very casual friends that are women they may see once in awhile, but deep, fulfilling interpersonal relationships generally do not exist for abusive women. When a man starts a new relationship, he should consider what this woman's relationship is like with other women.

Kayla was a young, beautiful woman who dated a series of young men and kept her distance emotionally from them. She would get to know a man and think she was falling in love and developing feelings for him, when abruptly she would stop dating him and move on to the next man. Kayla is not unlike many women who have their emotional guard up. Perhaps they have been hurt and are consciously or unconsciously seeking to maintain emotional distance.

There are many ways women may establish emotional distance in a relationship. She may begin to tell herself he has too many flaws, he is probably seeing other women, all men cheat, or other negative self-talk about him or men in general that allow her to pull back emotionally. She may begin to see more than one man at a time to keep disconnected. She may also spread out the amount of time she spends with one man; the infrequency of seeing each man will prevent her from building a strong emotional connection with anyone. She may lie and not tell the truth to any of these men so that she does not have an authentic connection. Men also do this to avoid emotional closeness and intimacy. The problem is they do not develop any real intimacy or connection with someone and continue to project a false sense of self. The disconnect they experience keeps them at a comfortable emotional distance.

Some of these women use diversions to avoid serious topics, or change the subject and often turn the focus on him when he asks her about herself. While emotional guardedness is not an abusive behavior in itself, it can be frustrating and debilitating in a relationship, and a woman who is extremely emotionally guarded may limit any emotional support or intimacy a man will receive. If a woman has not dealt with her trauma, she may be unintentionally emotionally neglectful and may lack meaningful communication. The neglect she may show a man is likely not her intention; rather, it is merely a defense. Nevertheless, good intentions do nothing to fill the void the man feels when he is essentially ignored on an emotional level. If they are intentionally neglectful and unwilling to look at how the trauma they experienced is affecting their man, there may be an abusive motive behind their behavior.

It is important to find out how they feel about being close and connected with someone. Sometimes, someone may enter relationships knowing their trauma has impacted them and purposely wanting to address it so that it does not affect the relationship. If this is the case, there is hope for the relationship. A man will want someone who acknowledges this and is willing to change. A conversation about their trauma and how it was resolved may give reassurance that she is ready to connect on an emotional level. I advise men to find out how much resolution their partners have experienced from their trauma. Did they go to counseling? What are they willing to do immediately to find healing and resolution for their past experience? Are they willing to speak to a counselor and move forward, or are they denying any impact from the trauma and minimizing the man's concerns regarding intimacy?

If they are minimizing these concerns regarding intimacy, then the man is likely headed down a long road of emotional neglect with no clear indication of when it will ever change.

Unrealistic Expectations

The abused man is in a "constant state of failure" with no encouragement or loving words from his abuser. Jeff said he felt beat down constantly by the words of his wife who never appreciated or encouraged him. Most of the men I have interviewed have said the same thing. The message they received, whether spoken or unspoken, was that they would never measure up and are just not good enough. Men in this predicament get the message that they never get anything right, and without their partner, they are nothing. These unrealistic expectations are expressed abusively in angry, harsh words and some abusers do this intentionally, while some do not realize they are doing it. It is like the man I interviewed who came home one day so excited about the meaningful day he had. When he came home, he wanted to share with his wife how things had turned out that day. He excitedly told her about his day and all of the things that had gone so well for him. He looked at her in anticipation of her saying something like, "That is great Honey." Instead she looked at him and replied, "Well, too bad you are still getting old and going bald." He said he was floored as this venomous comment flowed out of her mouth with all its intended cruelty.

Now, only she knows her motives or why exactly she expressed her anger that way toward her husband, but I would tend to think she did not want him to feel good. It was as though she was disgusted with him. Just like the saying, "misery loves company," when an abusive woman is not feeling good about herself and her life, she will not want her partner to either. She will want him to feel as unhappy and miserable as she is feeling. In this case, she used one sentence to knock him down emotionally and subsequently felt better about herself in the process.

When we are in an intimate relationship with someone, there is a level of power that comes to both parties by way of *mutual vulnerability*. When one's love language is abusive, there can be the expression of power without vulnerability. The person doing the abusing is not revealing their vulnerability or openness; instead, they are demanding compliance with their will and expressing their power in the relationship. At times, the abuser may show vulnerability, but this is generally not in a healthy way. In contrast, in a healthy relationship, one's openness and vulnerability can bring great closeness like nothing previously experienced.

The joy of a truly intimate relationship where there is love and understanding is unlike any other experience we will have in this life. It is a truly remarkable and fulfilling experience, and one everyone deserves. Love in the highest sense can be intoxicating, breathtaking, consuming, spiritual, and filled with so much satisfaction on every level. But in an abusive relationship, this vulnerability associated with the abuser's power and demands has the striking ability to hurt us at our very core.

The people we let into our "vulnerable spot" can heal or harm. When someone is using this vulnerability against us, it damages us physically, mentally, and emotionally. This can lead victims of abuse to feel tired and drained when they are around their spouse or partner.

In practice, I often will ask people to think about how they feel when they are around their partner. Do they feel cared for and loved? Do they have energy and feel good about themselves? Or are they drained and have a negative impression and attitude toward themselves? When we are around those we love that we in turn know love us, there is generally a positive energy that exists. While this positive energy is not always present due to life stresses and day-to-day pressures, it is an underlying current that exists in a relationship where both parties are looking out for the best interest of themselves and their partners. However, if we are around someone who wants us to feel bad about ourselves or does not have our best interest at heart, we often feel drained and exhausted. It is important for our well-being to have people in our lives that believe in us, support us, and want the best for us. Remember, this is not just in words, but in action. *Action* is the key to identifying truly loving behavior. If they are being told they are not good enough, and that they are a failure, causing them to feel horrible or bad about themselves, they may be with an abusive woman.

It is important for them to gain perspective and really pay attention to their interactions with this person and how their vulnerability within the relationship is impacting them. If it is negatively impacting them, they may want to make their personal well-being a priority and make some life changes.

The Empty Void
Some abusive women will be a bottomless pit of attention-seeking behavior. They will constantly

desire never-ending reassurance. She will demand so much attention because it will be the only validation she has. If the man spends a lot of time and attention on her, and she still does not think it is enough, she could have an emotional vacuum. For instance, it is normal in any relationship where intimacy is building for time and effort to go into that relationship. Many times men think this intimacy will just happen or that a woman will be satisfied with little investment. The truth is that in any healthy relationship, it is required that one invests sufficient time and effort. There are no shortcuts to avoid the investment of time it takes to build a lasting, genuine, and strong relationship. The idea of quality time consisting of rare and few occasions is not going to build any kind of relationship of any real substance.

For most women, if there is no time-investment made on the part of the man, the relationship will fade and she will find other opportunities and options because she is seeking what is best for her. A man cannot find fault in this. However, if a woman has much of her man's time and she still is not satisfied, she may have an emotional void. Not all abusive women have this characteristic; however, this is present many times in the women I work with and have personally counseled who admit to being abusive toward their partners.

Whenever I am talking about abuse characteristics, I am talking about extremes in behavior. With this characteristic, I am talking about an extreme sense of emptiness that is only filled when a woman's partner is around. She is miserable and unhappy if he is not present and always available to her at any given moment. It is this imbalance in her emotional needs that constitutes a risk factor for abuse. As she seeks to have all of their man's attention, she will exclude all of his friends, as well as all outside activities he enjoys. As he seeks to give her more and more attention, he will give up all his outside interests and become focused on her exclusively, which creates the vacuum the relationship will begin to exist in that is simply unsustainable. The pressure of this will cause the relationship to implode and can result in expressed hostility by both parties.

A well-rounded woman will have outside interests she is involved with, friends she spends time with, and hobbies that she participates in so that it will not be about the man all the time. This is good and healthy, and men who are dating should encourage this in their women. He should find out what she does with her free time. Does she go out to lunch with the girls? Does she have fun things to do when he is not around?

A balance of interests and fulfilling endeavors in her life is crucial: it cannot be about him all the time. If everything revolves around the man, he will begin to feel suffocated and resentful, and she will in turn become resentful of him and his inability to "make her happy." If a man is dating a woman who has a healthy need for attention, he will not feel overwhelmed and frustrated by the desire for attention. Conversely, if a man is with a woman who has an emotional vacuum, this is not something unchangeable in a relationship. To instigate change, he should encourage a sense of balance, and discuss this with the woman in his life. He can help her to find her own interests and to develop herself in a positive way that will benefit the relationship. Ultimately, it is all about what the couple wants in terms of the amount of attention given and received in the relationship.

Possessive Control

Another indication of potential abusive control can be when someone is very possessive. They know everything about you, and can describe what your day is like in a play-by-play. They know where you go at night, and how long it takes you to get to work and home. For some relationships, it is okay for a person to know each detail of the other's day. The important point is if it is welcomed by both parties and if it is used as a means to maintain control of the other person. If it becomes about control, then it is a risk factor toward abuse. If this is a risk factor, the woman will want to know every detail of every day; in fact, any unknowns create intense anxiety and insecurity. This type of woman is fuelled by a feeling of helplessness that drives her desire to feel like she has some control over her man. The anxiety she has drives her to scrutinize his every move.

This woman will think about him obsessively all day. The focus on him masks the emptiness she feels. He is her everything. A woman who becomes obsessive is looking for the man to fill the *emotional void* she feels. She becomes so focused on the man and begins to place the responsibility of her happiness on him. This burden is tough for anyone to bear. She may call him five or six times a day to check in and see how he is doing. If a woman calls a man she is in a relationship with a couple times a day, there is no need to become paranoid. However, if she is calling him *throughout* the day *all* day, one has to wonder why. If it resembles a time clock with a punch card, he may be under a little too much scrutiny. She believes that he will fail her, so anxiety drives her to stay on top of his every move so he does not have a chance to betray her. She may even know it is irrational, but will still follow his every move through every day

If a man is not comfortable with the level of information she has about him and his whereabouts, he needs to set some boundaries. If he does not want her calling him all day, he needs to have this candid conversation. A good therapist may help her to deal with her issues that are causing her to act controlling and possessive. Kayla, the woman I spoke of earlier, would monitor her boyfriend so much that she knew where he was almost every minute of every day. She would harass him if he was even a few minutes late from work, and would accuse him of leaving early so he could be with another woman. She was truly convinced that in the twenty minutes it took for him to come home, he had enough time to run by someone's house and have sex with them before rushing home. The paranoia and hyper-vigilance was a self-protective measure. While she wanted love and reassurance, her boyfriend became very tired of her constant scrutiny and internally withdrew emotionally. It is clear that there is an element of paranoia that exists in her mind. If he glances at a woman walking by, she deduces he must want to sleep with her. If he is a minute late, he must be cheating. These irrational and destructive beliefs stem from the extreme anxiety and the thoughts they create in her mind. She feels she will catch him if it is the last thing she does. If a man has cheated or is cheating on his wife or girlfriend, then the paranoia she feels may not be all in her head, so it is important for him to be candid about his actions also. I have talked to men who have said, "I have no idea why she calls me twenty times a day at work," and when I ask if they have ever cheated, they sheepishly reply, "well yeah, I cheated with a co-worker last year but I am not doing it anymore." My response to them is that while they are not doing it anymore, it does not mean their wife or girlfriend has gained trust again. I then give them a recommendation to couples counseling to begin to heal the relationship. However, if a man has not cheated and his partner is still experiencing paranoia and high anxiety, he may be with a woman who feels out of control in her own life and who responds with a need to control him to protect her from being abandoned.

The Jealous Rages
Jealousy, the beast within that consumes and creates fire within one's heart and mind
Kimberly Taylor

The power of jealousy can be frightening. Jealousy is a component of possessive control. In many of the old myths, jealousy was a fire that drove people to do things they would never imagine or believe they were capable of. The power of jealousy can be daunting, yet it is an emotion that we all have felt. So, when does it cross the line? Is it okay to be jealous when someone you love is interested in someone else? Is it okay to be jealous when your girlfriend or boyfriend gets hit on in front of you? What makes jealousy wrong or extreme? I remember watching a 20/20 program where they conducted a hidden camera test that examined jealousy in relationships. They staged a scene where a couple went out for dinner and a male/female waiter was instructed to flirt obnoxiously with the woman/man. The woman/man who was being hit on knew that this was taking place. The social experiment was to see how the other person would react to someone obnoxiously flirting with their spouse or partner. It was interesting to see how the men and women responded. The truth is they were equally jealous and they did not like the fact that someone was paying this kind of attention to their partner. Some of them even confronted the waiter or waitress. It was interesting to watch them go from mild amusement to anger as these waiters became increasingly blatant. A few couples even found it funny at first but later became angry.

It is human to feel jealous sometimes. But when does it cross the line? What is not okay? When a woman's anger language includes a pattern of jealousy, she is jealous about everything. She may be jealous of your relationship with your children, your mother, or your friends. She may be jealous and make a scene if you even look at another woman. Her jealousy will be misplaced, out of context, and, at times, uncontrollable. She may even hit or slap you because she thinks you were with another woman.

This jealousy can become quite paranoid and the woman may imagine things in her head that have no basis in reality. This is quite clearly when you have the signs of jealousy that has risen to abuse. I remember one group I was facilitating for women abusers, and one petite blonde, no more than five foot four inches and not more than 120 pounds, told her story without hesitation. She had checked her boyfriend's phone and found a number she was not familiar with. She interpreted that to mean he was cheating on her. She said she was so enraged and jealous that she proceeded to put his head through a plate-glass window. She was subsequently arrested on felony charges of domestic violence. She served time in jail and was ordered into a 52 week batterer's treatment program. Her problem was that she would immediately react to any thoughts she had. She could have asked him about the number and discussed it calmly. Even if it was a girl's number, she had other choices she could have made. She didn't have to resort to violence. Sometimes the best decision is to face what one sees and accept you cannot change another person. It may mean walking away from the relationship.

However, this girl had learned violence was the answer by the abuse she saw growing up in her own family. She admitted to having an inability to control her emotions, gauge her anger, and show self-control.

Nevertheless, she did a lot of hard work and I am pleased to report that by the end of the group, she had gained a lot of self-control and was no longer attacking her boyfriend, who stayed with her.

If there are jealous rages in your relationship, you may be in jeopardy physically. It is very important to address jealousy if it is out of proportion and includes paranoid. Remember the danger associated with extreme jealousy and seek help and counseling when needed.

High Impulsivity

Abusive women will tend to have low impulse control. This may show itself in the abuse of substances such as illicit drugs, alcohol, or prescription medication. It has been my experience in practice that they tend to also have a tendency toward addiction such as sex addiction, food addiction, or compulsive and out-of-control spending habits.

Their impulsivity is demonstrated in their day-to-day behavior. If a woman has a substance abuse history and other impulsive behaviors, there is a greater risk for abusive behavior. How do they handle money, sex, food, alcohol, and medication? Are they excessive spenders with no apparent restraint? With sex, many women who have impulse control issues will have a lot of one-night stands and will engage in risky sexual behavior. They may also have problems with food, and may seek to use food to fill their emptiness in an impulsive way. They may even use pain medication in a way to numb their feelings and help them to level their moods. Do they seem to have self-control over their moods and their frustration level, or do they lack control and get frustrated easily? Their moods may switch from happy to sad and back again in a short period of time. The low impulse control can express itself with intense reactive anger where they fly off the handle for no apparent reason. They act now and think later. It has been my experience that women who have high levels of impulsivity in several of these areas may at times react with impulsive anger and physical abuse where they lack control over their emotions. Self-control is very hard for them when dealing with many areas of their life, which can be a warning sign of an abusive female.

Anger and Rage

At the heart of every abusive woman or man is unresolved anger. Unresolved anger is one of the most prevalent characteristics of an abusive woman. Anger tends to stem from the idea that others have mistreated, devalued, harmed, or in some way hurt the person who is experiencing the anger. While anger is a valid human emotion and is justified when one has been injured or harmed, the issue arises when this emotion simmers and becomes unresolved. Unresolved anger is very damaging to individuals and those they are close to. If a man is in a relationship with someone that has unresolved anger, he may find himself on the receiving end of much of the emotional expression. When someone has not dealt with this emotion, it will come out in many different forms with those who are near them. Perhaps the person feels cheated somehow or feels they are entitled to more than they have received. Underlying this feeling of discontent is a base of dissatisfaction and anger.

The emotion of anger has layers of hurt, sadness, frustration, and depression. One man I interviewed said his wife constantly told him how much he disappointed her and that she wished she had married someone else instead. They usually choose to do this at the most strategic moment when the man is already feeling down or when they are seeking some level of control. Matthew, who I interviewed, was trying very hard to work on his marriage, and awoke early one morning to make a beautiful breakfast for his wife. He had gone to the store and bought a dozen roses and made the table very special for his spouse. He said he wanted to show her how much he loved her and he wanted to have a fresh start for his marriage. That evening they got in a disagreement about something and he reminded her that he had made a huge effort that morning. Her response was a cold, "I expect those things. All the men I have dated have done those things for me." "She did not appreciate what I did for her," he said in total hopelessness. At the core of this is unresolved anger and mean spiritedness. She is displacing on him anger for her own frustration that life is not entirely what she wanted. Instead of looking within and trying to create some happiness for herself, she believes and feels he is supposed to "make her happy." When he does not live up to that, as no human being can, she is angry and frustrated, and all the disappointments in her life come to land solely on him. So many men have said, "I tried everything I could to make her happy, and she just always found a reason to be angry." They think it is something they are not doing. They try so hard until finally they realize it has nothing to do with them and really has everything to do with her and her own inability to find happiness within. An angry woman is angry because everything is everyone else's fault. She has not gained the insight that allows her to take responsibility for what happens in life.

Rage is different than anger. Rage is an overwhelming feeling that takes control of a person's emotions and actions. The difference between rage and anger is that anger is a manageable emotion, one in which someone has a choice, whereas rage is an all-consuming state. Many times, a woman or man who experiences rage will say that something the person whom they were angry with did brought on physical symptoms, such as shaking, trembling, and blurred vision, because it triggered a vivid memory tied to something from the past that was extremely traumatic or painful, possibly from childhood. This is by far the most dangerous form of anger, and if one is experiencing this form of anger or being the recipient of it, they must get help as soon as possible. This is the type of anger that can potentially end up in homicide. The person experiencing this type of anger can dissociate and do thing they did not know they were capable of. There are prisons filled with men and women who have killed their partners because of an episode of uncontrollable rage.

The Character/Personality Disorders and Abusive Women

I cannot talk about abusive women or abusive men at any length without talking about personality disorders. For the purpose of this chapter, I will focus on two of these disorders that from my experience are the most prevalent among the women I have treated who have been perpetrators of abuse. Many abusive women are also histrionic and anti-social; however, the ones I have seen most frequently in my practice are Narcissistic Personality Disorder (NPD) and Borderline Personality disorder (BPD).

The old myth of Narcissus and Echo is a tale of a nymph who falls in love with Narcissus, as does many of the other nymphs in the town. However, Narcissus is not in love with any of them. He goes and sits down by a pool of water and becomes enamored with his own reflection. The reflection he sees is so interesting and handsome that he falls in love with it. And so the creation of the narcissist began. The myth has a man as its main character, but studies show that many of those who have NPD are women. Someone who has a narcissistic personality is one who is often inwardly focused and self-obsessed. They see other people as an extension of themselves whose purpose is to serve and fulfill their needs and desires. They do not consider the feelings of the other person. They can be bitingly cruel and demeaning, and can leave people bewildered and dismayed at their callous ways. One minute, they are so in love with the man and he can do nothing wrong, and the next, he is being discarded with the trash pickup. Those who have been in relationships with narcissists will tell you it is one of the most damaging and emotionally devastating experiences they have had. The stunning coldness is so disconcerting, it leaves people very hurt and betrayed. It is also a hard disorder to treat, and long-term treatment is therefore the general method of choice for most therapists and psychologists treating a patient who has NPD.

Each of the men I interviewed described their wives with many of the characteristics and behavior of NPD. Jeff talked about his wife telling him how much she hated him on a regular basis, and how he was never a real man. Matthew was working 60 hours a week and one day came home to his wife announcing she was going to Europe with her daughter for a month and he cannot come. When he then said he wanted to talk about it and may want to go, she vehemently tried to shame him by calling him selfish for not just letting her go on a whim to Europe for a month. This is narcissistic behavior. They are only thinking about themselves to the complete exclusion of the feelings of the other person in the relationship. Can they be helped? Yes. Do they truly want help? This is the deciding question, as their sense of entitlement may overshadow any desire to change or a recognition that they need help.

Many abusers can have Borderline Personality Disorder. This is because the nature of this disorder lends itself to extremes in behavior, high risk-taking behavior, and a propensity for extreme anger. They have a hard time controlling and regulating their emotions, which can make them feel overwhelmed when experiencing intense emotional states. One woman I counseled said she felt a huge swell of heat all over her body when she got mad, and it was as if she had to release it by hitting something or someone. She had been very abusive to her partner and wanted to get better and have a healthy relationship, but she just felt she could not control her emotions. When someone has BPD, intensive therapy is so important as it allows them to learn some emotional regulation, which can help them to avoid reacting impulsively to every emotion. They can be helped if they want the help, and are willing to do the hard work that goes along with getting that help. I never say that someone is hopeless. The only thing that precludes someone from getting help is if they do not want it.

The process of anger for women is different than that of men, and we must understand their underlying experiences, traumas, and beliefs to understand their anger.

CHAPTER 8
The Wounded Abuser

Kayla is a young twenty-five year old who has had so much life experience for her age that she can quickly size people up within minutes of meeting them. She does this because she had to learn the skill early on in life to feel safe. Kayla is tall and slender with long legs and long brown hair. She has a captivating smile, and when she walks into a room, men's heads turn. They pay attention to her because she is strikingly pretty. She is also very quick witted and tends to be attracted to men who are "bad boys." Kayla is drawn to the drama in their lives in a way that she doesn't even understand. In fact, most of the men she is attracted to have other relationships or recent ex-girlfriends that never fully leave the scene.

When Kayla dates a man, she loves the attention she gets, and it becomes her only focus. She idealizes her male romances from the onset and soaks up all the overwhelming attention that comes in the beginning. Sex becomes a part of the relationship early on as well. Kayla feels validated by every word her men say to her and how much they like her. But her expectations are unrealistic, and she can quickly alienate boyfriends due to her neediness. For instance, she calls them constantly and interprets everything they say in every text or call as a rejection of her. Kayla indeed feels like a bottomless pit for attention and control.

Kayla is waiting for the other shoe to drop, and because she knows it will drop, she is protecting herself from all angles. As an example of this strategy, she dates several men at once and keeps them all at a distance. She sees a couple of them irregularly and spreads out the time in between visits so she doesn't grow close with any of them. Then there is one whom she sees often and considers her primary relationship. To see her and to know her, one would wonder why she is so insecure. Why is she is drawn by intense anxiety to monitor the man in her life? And why does she unconsciously sabotage any real hope at true intimacy? However, when we learn a little more about Kayla's history, we can gain some understanding as to why she is this way.

Kayla was born into a family with a single mother. She has one brother and two sisters who are all much older. With these as her family members, Kayla grew up in a home with no money and very little security of any kind. It was so bad that her basic needs were rarely met for food, shelter, and clothing. For this reason, she began to distrust the world around her. Kayla even had high anxiety about being abandoned as a child, so she developed panic attacks. Then she started relationships with boys at a very young age and looked to them for love. But she didn't want to be loved only for her body or strictly because of what she could do for them.

Over time, this type of behavior became a way of life for Kayla. She went from one boyfriend to the next and soon began to mask her pain with alcohol. But after she had turned twenty, she thought she met "Mr. Right." He was very good to her at first, and they enjoyed each other and had fun times together. She subsequently introduced him to her son and thought that he was definitely the one for her. However, Kayla later found out that he was using drugs and craftily hiding it from everyone.

Several months into the relationship, "Mr. Right" got mad because he saw a number on her cell phone that he didn't recognize. In a rage he suddenly pushed her to the ground and smashed his foot into her face while stomping on her. But Kayla managed to escape. She ran out of the house with her face bleeding and went over to the neighbors so she could call the police. The police arrived quickly, but while they looked around to arrest Kayla's boyfriend, he fled. Despite this drama, Kayla stayed with her man. Rather than breaking up, she went through this cycle of abuse with him several times until one day he almost killed her by choking her. Kayla finally got away from him after some time, yet the scars from that experience remained very painful.

Kayla never went for counseling after that experience. Instead, she just kept moving into other relationships. She thought that her next relationship was love at first sight. They got along very well and had a great time together whenever they went out, so they eventually began to do everything together. They started having passionate sex, and he was so loving that she felt truly cared for by this new man. Kayla "knew" that they would be together forever. Then they moved in together—which is when things began to change. She started to catch him in little lies. This provoked extreme anxiety in her so that she began to obsess over him and monitor his every move. Kayla would call him twenty times a day, and if he didn't pick up right away, he was in big trouble. When she called, she would check constantly to find out where he was and what he was doing.

Kayla also noticed that everything he did began to irritate her. She started yelling at him and telling him she hated him. They could not be in a room together for ten minutes without her provoking a fight and yelling and screaming or hitting him. She would pound him in the face and yell at him. He would leave and minutes later she would call him and try to get him to return home. This went on for months. During this time, they stopped having sex and her boyfriend withdrew emotionally because she was so violent with him. He ended up having a relationship with a girl from work and Kayla eventually found out. This led to months and months of fighting, cheating, and intense anger that never left. There were only brief moments of peace and kindness to each other. She believes they truly had love for each other but they each participated in the destruction of the relationship. They each went down the road of negativity and allowed it to overwhelm the love they had for each other. Kayla and her boyfriend tried for a couples years to work it out after that but the fights and yelling and hitting never stopped between them and it led to the final demise of their relationship.

She had terrible mood swings and a fierce temper, which she admits she felt no control of. She said she tried to control herself but felt totally lost and helpless. She truly felt no resolution was possible. She knew she needed to get control of herself and she decided to get therapy. She was finally ready to talk about the past, the abuse, the men, the substance use, the violence that had been done to her and the violence she herself committed. She was ready to acknowledge she had to make good choices for herself and her life.

Kayla is an example of someone very traumatized at an early age that internalizes and then projects the hurt and anger onto those she comes in contact with. The saying, "hurt people, HURT people," fits her. She was once a victim and later became an abuser. Her boyfriend's infidelity was never justified, but neither was Kayla's violence. The good news is she really began to look at her behavior and her choices and started therapy. She found the strength and found the resources to get the help she needed and now she walks with her head held high and a peace in her life she never had before. She is no longer abusive to the men in her life. She made the decision and changed her life.

CHAPTER 9
The Socialite

Connie comes from a privileged background. She was raised with both parents and two siblings, a brother and a sister. She attended the best private schools money could buy, and her young life was full of excess. But she was lonely as a child because she spent much of her time with nannies. Her parents were too preoccupied and didn't have the time for her.

Learned Behavior

She saw early on that relationships were filled with violence by watching her parents throw things at one another, swear, and call each other every name known to man. She wondered if her parents ever really loved each other. They seemed so happy at times, yet even the happy moments were followed by violence. Connie learned early on you cannot trust anyone.

When she began dating in high school, she was always drawn toward the boys who she could gain from. She viewed relationships in a very calculating way. Essentially, she would say, "What can you do for me? What is in it for me?" Although she didn't say this aloud, she thought it, and she dated according to that very plan.

Effects

Despite such calculations, she was incredibly unstable emotionally. She had great mood swings in which she would feel extremely high and sort of invincible. When she was in these moods, she would be the life of the party. She would stay up for long periods of time and never seem to get tired. Yet she always came down from these moods, and every crash hit rock bottom. Connie would become very tired and resign herself to sleeping and avoiding personal contact. She would go for days without showering or speaking to anyone. She would become very irritable and angry over seemingly meaningless things.

When she got older and moved in with her boyfriend, she would go on spending sprees and plan extravagant vacations during her high moods. However, when she came down and began to feel depressed, she would focus on all the ways that her boyfriend was letting her down. He wasn't making enough money, he was never there, and he didn't seem to appreciate her. Her problems all became focused on her boyfriend.

The Cycle Continues

She sometimes thought he reminded her of her father, and she would get so angry at him she would slam her fists into his chest. He would look at her wide eyed and say, "Why are you doing this," but she would continue to hit him. When she felt she finally had all of her anger out, she would get up and walk away, feeling relieved and acting as if nothing had happened.

He would understandably get angry with her for hitting him, but she would dismiss it and say, "It was just a little argument we were having. You always make me so mad by pushing my buttons like my dad used to do." In her mind, it was a small thing, and she told herself she could never really hurt him; he was just too big. But the hitting continued, and she became more aggressive as he continued to be the focus of all that was wrong in her world. The idea of looking inward and having some insight was not part of Connie's reality.

Self-Medicating

Eventually, she began using prescription drugs to help with her moods. She took Percocet, Vicodin, Oxycontin, and any other painkiller she could get her hands on. She began taking a few a day but eventually increased to the point at which she wasn't sure how many pills she was taking. At one point she was taking about 30 pills a day. She hid this well from her boyfriend.

She began going out every night with girlfriends to bars and not coming home until 3 or 4 a.m. on a regular basis. At one point, she stopped coming home at all for days.

Falling Apart

The frequency of the fighting increased, and she could not go a day without hitting her boyfriend or emotionally battering him. It got so bad he told her he didn't love her anymore and that he was leaving her. She didn't believe him. However, several weeks later, in a very calm and cool manner, he packed his bags and walked out the door. Connie blamed him for abandoning her and claimed he was such a horrible man for leaving.

She filled herself with hate and anger and went out looking for her next "victim," who she would try and garner sympathy from because of the bad man who had just left her. She ended up finding a much older man with a lot of financial resources to take her and her party lifestyle on. However, several months in, he began to see through her motives and quickly exited the relationship, leaving her on the search for her next "victim."

Conclusion

The difference between Kayla and Connie is that, while they both were abusive toward their partners, Kayla recognized this and got the help and counseling she knew she needed. Kayla realized that she needed to work on herself and change the patterns that had become self defeating for her and her relationships.

Connie, however, had no insight. She never took any responsibility for her actions. Connie continued to blame her ex-boyfriend for all the wrong he did to her and never looked at her part in the relationship's demise. Both women had the same chance at a better and more fulfilling life, but one chose to remain the perceived victim while the other looked within and made herself better before damaging another person. She held herself responsible and got help.

CHAPTER 10
IPA on Children

Studies comparing children exposed to intimate partner violence to those who are not have found that children exposed to violence struggle more in life than those raised in non-violent homes. In the U.S., 3.3 million children ages 3 to 17 are at risk of exposure to intimate partner abuse, (Peter Jaffe, David Wolfe, and Susan Kaye Wilson (1990) "Children of Battered Women." Newbury Park, Ca: Sage Publications). In homes where IPA exists, children are abused at a rate of 1,500 times higher than the normal average (National Coalition Against Domestic Violence (1993) "Facts on Domestic Violence" (brochure) Washington D.C.) Furthermore, according to Dr. Bruce Perry, (childtrauma.org) medical problems such as heart disease and asthma can be directly attributed to childhood trauma in certain cases.

Dr. Perry found in his research that children who are exposed to trauma also have changes in their brain structure. Children who live in a violent environment learn to accept violence as a way to resolve conflict, and their brains concretely form themselves to handle stress less effectively than children from non-violent homes.

Parents I have worked with have observed some of the following behaviors in their children who were exposed to violence: temper tantrums, acting out aggressively at school, withdrawing and wanting to be alone, and crying frequently. Some children also reportedly feel guilty for the violence between their parents, or they may feel angry toward one or both parents.

Protective Factors

While all children exposed to violence and abuse will be affected in some way, there are some protective factors that have proven to insulate them from the extent of devastation they may experience. According to childwelfare.gov, formerly the National Clearinghouse on Child Abuse and Neglect, some of these factors include social competence, intelligence, high self-esteem, outgoing temperament, strong sibling and peer relationships, and a supportive relationship with an adult. The more of these strong connections they have with others, the more insulated they are.

The older the child, the more coping skills they generally have to alleviate stress brought on by IPA in their parents' relationship. It also appears that, the closer they are to the observation of an incident, the greater the level of anxiety. In other words, an incident observed last night would trigger greater anxiety than one observed several months or years prior. The more time that has passed, the less anxious they become.

The best protective factor is for there to be no exposure to abuse or violence and for the child to see love, respect, and peace modeled in their home from whoever is caring for them.

What Can I Do to Help My Child?

I have spoken with parents who feel guilty about the abuse their children witnessed in the home, and they are very concerned that the children will carry these scars forever and possibly end up in abusive relationships similar to theirs.

It is important to put forth best efforts and get the necessary help to alleviate as much of the distress and trauma as one can. Here are a few things to do if a child has been exposed to abuse and violence in their parents' relationship.

Have Open Dialogue with the Child

The first and most important thing is to create a dialogue with the child. How does the child view his or her relationship with both parents? How do they feel about what they observed? Children can view things in unexpected ways. Many times their perspective is more fearful then one may think because they're trying to build a knowledge base with missing pieces and false information.

If a parent feels they have a good grasp and understanding about how to approach their child, then they may be able to do this on their own. However, in most cases, the family would benefit from involving a children's therapist.

A therapist can more effectively ask the child how they feel about what they have observed (remember: what they feel is real to them). The parent may be very surprised at what is revealed. Some children form strong memories, while others have minimal recall.

In either case, the parent may need to answer some questions and fill in the blanks for the therapist. Conversation with a child should be age appropriate—the things said to a five year old would not be the same as what is said to a teenager—and the therapist can assist with preparing both child and parent so that the discussion is beneficial and not harmful in any way.

It is very important to separate the behavior from the person. Avoid bad-mouthing the other parent. Instead, talk about the fact that sometimes good people behave badly. One can talk about choices versus the root character of the person. They can discuss what the difference is between loving behavior and abusive behavior and how it is a choice that is made. This will help the child to understand the care and love felt for that person while also acknowledging the behavior. <u>If a parent degrades or calls another parent a name in front of a child or to a child, they are hurting the child. The child who loves that parent will feel attacked and hurt if said parent is being put down.</u>

It is important to give accurate information while protecting the child from further harm. The older the child, the more cognitive ability they have to process information, and the more they can understand. The most important thing to remember, though, is that their perspective is their reality. Make sure they know they have a safe place they can always go when they need to talk about anything on their mind no matter how hard or horrible they think it may be.

Help the Child to See Healthy Relationships Modeled

One of the very best things a parent can do for their child is to model a healthy relationship with them and with those in their life. Children learn by what they see, and if they witness their parents in a loving relationship, they will learn how to emulate that. This is truly the best and most effective way to teach children about healthy relationships. I have heard men say, "I learned to treat a woman by watching my dad and how he treated my mom." Others have said that they saw their mothers being beaten on a regular basis and felt helpless and confused with great anger at their fathers, yet love for them. A few have said that they promised themselves they would never do to their wives what they saw their fathers do.

Frequently however, I heard them say, "I didn't want to be like my dad, but I grew up and did the same thing and ended up hitting my wife." In the work I have done with men that had solid role models in their fathers, where they saw love demonstrated alongside the absence of abuse, there is a greater ability to follow in these footsteps. A strong foundation to a healthy relationship includes: commitment, trust, honesty, faithfulness, communication, affection, and respect. The very best insulator for a child is to help them understand what **true love** is through word and action.

Remember: We Are Not Perfect

It is very important for parents to show their humanity with their children and to demonstrate how to live life without being "perfect." Many parents are so hard on themselves and live in constant guilt over any parenting shortcomings. We are human and by nature have frailties.

A parent that mimics perfection to their child, without showing any faults, is not helping their child. Children need to see someone who tries hard to do the best they can as a parent and loves them in the process. They need to hear, "I'm sorry," and "I was wrong; I didn't make the best decision about this." It is okay to admit our failures at times and to acknowledge them is helpful to our children. As they see imperfection modeled, they can trust in their own abilities and learn from their failures in a way that will make them better individuals.

Encourage Activities for your Child

Remember that it is not a child's job to take care of a parent. It is not healthy for them to be expected to take on the role of an adult to make sure their parent is emotionally okay. If a child seems too focused on the concerns of their parent, the parent should make an effort to get them involved with their friends, sports, school activities, and other things they enjoy so their parent's "adult problems" don't become their problems. Children are not equipped to deal with the things that adults must deal with in everyday life, and they should not have to babysit their parents.

The Teen Years

What happens when children become teens and they have not resolved the abuse they have been exposed to or that they have learned is acceptable? Many times the cycle of abuse begins to be perpetuated when the child enters the teen years. One in three teens experience some form of IPA during their high school years. Many of these teens report coming from homes where they observed violent behavior.

Problems Coping

In one study, 85% of the children witnessing domestic violence admitted to a drinking problem which started as early as 11, and 2% began drinking at age 9 (Children in the Crossfire: Violence in the home. How does it affect our child? Health Communications, Inc. 53-164). The feelings teens begin to experience in relation to others can be scary and overwhelming. This is compounded by the lack of skills they may have in expressing themselves and handling anger and frustration.

An Advocate's Point of View

According to Gina Graham, a domestic violence advocate for teens, the boys she had spoken to who had experienced dating abuse made reference to issues of control, extreme jealousy, and threats. "The threats from the girls were typically about harming themselves if the boyfriend would not stay in the relationship," she stated. "It would become emotional blackmail, and the boys felt helpless to get out of their relationships. The young men said they didn't know who to talk to about it. They were typically very concerned the young woman would follow through with a suicide threat, and consequently, they felt a lot of pressure to stay in the relationship." Additionally, the boys were often told they could only spend limited time with their friends. Teenagers sometimes have jealousy they do not know how to control, and so they may seek to manipulate their partner's activities and social lives to feel some false sense of control.

The more they suffocate their partner, the more their partner begins to resent them, and the vicious cycle continues. "Teens are not equipped to handle the heavy emotions they are experiencing at such a young age in these early relationships," Gina said.

She also said that she saw a lot of emotional insecurity. "Many of the abusive females I spoke with did not know that, when you are angry with your boyfriend, it is not okay to lash out and put your hands on them.

"Many of them, in an attempt to get their way, begin cursing and confronting and yelling at their boyfriends. Many of these girls don't know how to handle other relationships very well, either. They are typically the ones confronting their friends and classmates and showing an inability to handle conflict."

Conclusion

What we are hearing is that many teens do not learn the skills needed to communicate and express themselves, and they find themselves overwhelmed with new emotions when they begin new relationships resulting in acting out in ways that are abusive and controlling.

Parents can begin to teach their children about relationships from a very early age, and as a result, they can grow up knowing how to communicate and effectively deal with relationships with friends and those of the opposite sex.

CHAPTER 11
WHY MEN STAY

How often have we heard people say, "I have no idea why she stays with him; he treats her horribly." Well, the same can be said for the man. Their reasons for staying are as many and as complex as women's. From the outside, one can questions and wonder why a person would stay and endure any form of abuse. However, we can never truly understand the hurt and the pain he or she goes through and cannot fully grasp the reasons someone would endure this type of treatment. Whether it happens suddenly in an explosive outburst or in a progressively slow fashion, abuse is a very traumatic experience and should never be minimized. I will look at each of these reasons individually and try to relay the perspective I have heard from those I have interviewed.

The Children

All the things that fathers rehearse in their head about the children and the dilemma of leaving includes the following:

- Divorce is bad for kids
- I'll wait for the kids to get older
- I'm afraid to leave them with her
- I'm afraid I won't be able to get custody
- I'm afraid she won't let me see the kids because she'll have control over visitation (threats)
- She won't care for the kids appropriately when I am gone
- I am not sure I am ready to be a single dad.

There is a strong concern in these men about how the divorce will impact their children. I have talked to dads who have said that their wives are good mothers, despite being abusive to them, yet they fear the devastation the children will experience from the divorce. Children are impacted by divorce and they are impacted by observing their parents being abusive toward one another. There is no easy answer here. Statistics show that 80 to 90 percent of children who grow up in homes where they observe domestic violence will become either abusive or the recipient of abuse in their adult years. The impact on children is far reaching. (Rosen, 2004) Many children who grow up in violent homes suffer trauma-related conditions including PTSD, developmental delays, and other serious issues. Dr.

Bruce Perry (childtrauma.org) has done extensive research on domestic violence and the effect viewing it has on. He shows in very detailed studies on his website how a child's brain development is significantly impacted by observing violence in the home. A large percentage of children who observe domestic violence get PTSD and suffer from behavioral disorders, anxiety, phobias, depressive disorders, and failure in school. Children exposed to ongoing violence are at risk for impaired emotional, social, cognitive, and physiological problems. Many fathers are not aware of the impact that the violence is having on their children, and once they learn of the impact, they vow to do something different to not expose their children to this harmful traumatic experience. The impact of observing domestic violence in the home is so far reaching it increases the child's risk rather than inoculating them against later psychopathology. Despite the significant impact that observation of violence in the home has on children, one can also not neglect the impact that divorce has upon the family. Divorce does impact children, and decisions related to their care should be given much thought and careful consideration. However, it is very important to recognize the serious impact that observing abuse has on them.

If one decides to get out, I recommend counseling for yourself and your children to understand and cope with loss, anger, sadness, and the other emotions that come with making this step in your life. I also recommend reading as many resources as you can about parenting and healing after divorce. It will become critical to be the best parent you can be remembering that you will not have any control over what the other person does or how they will parent. It is very important to have good communication with children and to speak to them about things as is appropriate for their age. A counselor can be a good guide with some of these topics and can tell a concerned parent what is appropriate and how to discuss it. One mistake many parents make is assuming their child is fine because they are not showing behavioral symptoms after the divorce or after observing violence. Children cope differently and the one who is showing few signs could be the one in the most pain.

Religious Guilt

Many men enter marriage with the very sincere hope that this will be the final phase of their lives, and that they will remain with their spouse for the long term. Similar to many women, they take their vows and their commitment seriously and hold dear that it was a commitment made before God. These men come from many different faiths. They enter their marriage with the intent to stick to the vow, "'til death do us part." Their spiritual beliefs and values are very strong and compelling reasons they stay in abusive marriages. They believe there is something they can and should do to make the marriage right, and to help her stop her bad behavior. The religious guilt can be a powerful deterrent from escaping an abusive situation. For many, the guilt of leaving outweighs the misery of the abuse suffered, and so they choose to suffer in silence. Many counselors of different faiths have stated that from a spiritual standpoint, it is God who does not desire that anyone suffer abuse at the hands of their partner.

I have personally counseled many women who have stayed in abusive marriages because their pastor, priest or clergy member told them it was the right thing to do to continue in the marriage, despite the detriment to their lives and the lives of their children. The advice I give to women about staying in an abusive relationship, I also give to men. I advocate for physical and emotional safety for anyone in an abusive situation.

Sometimes a person will be advised to, "stay and pray," by a well-meaning clergy member. What they do not realize in giving this advice is that these victims could be seriously injured or killed at the hands of their abuser during this time they were told to stick it out. If people do not want to end the relationship, they can separate and remain at a distance from their abuser while maintaining their security.

It really is a matter of, "wait and see" what changes take place. The victim should remain safe and watch what action the abusive person takes toward getting better and changing his or her behavior. Many clergy are providing this type of wise counsel when they are confronted with abuse within their churches, and this approach provides the best opportunity for safety. Sometimes divorce is the only answer, and one should not feel guilty for making a choice to remain safe and protected.

I remember speaking to a pastor about men who are abused by women. The pastor laughed and said, "Oh, any man can fight off a woman; you have to be kidding me, men are not abused." I found it very disturbing that he was dismissing and minimizing abuse against men, yet appeared concerned about abuse against women. It made me wonder how many men in his very church were abused and would never speak to him about it because his attitude permeated his demeanor.

I have planned conferences about intimate partner abuse along with clergy and police departments. It is not uncommon for a pastor to call me or send someone to my practice who attends his or her church and is experiencing IPA.

One man said he stayed because he wanted his children to know and respect their faith and their family. He had been raised with a strong faith and wanted to have his family stick together. What he did not realize is the damage that was happening to his children when they observed their mother hit their father and demean him on a regular basis. They would see her abusive toward their father during the week, and then on Sunday, she became a very loving and different person. The children saw that at home and behind closed doors it was okay to be abusive, and on Sunday you acted like the world was beautiful and everyone was happy. As a result, these children learned hypocrisy in behavior and how to fake how one presents him or herself to the world. One child said this turned him away from his faith for some time growing up.

One man who sought to "do the right thing and remain married" felt so guilty at the idea of divorce that he endured years of physical abuse at the hands of his wife. Finally, when his grandmother was on her deathbed, she said it was okay for him to divorce his wife. He had never discussed his abuse with his grandmother, but knew she was aware of what he was going through. He said he felt a huge sense of relief by her words.

Subsequently, his wife had gone to see their priest to discuss their marital issues. After the meeting, the priest contacted him concerned and asked him to come in and see him as soon as he could. When they met, the priest was adamant that the man could not go back to his house and live with his wife. He told him he was not safe to go back to his own house. The priest was concerned that she would violently harm him, perhaps in front of his children.

It was such an impacting meeting that he cried in the priest's office from relief and from the acknowledgement that he was not safe. He had not felt safe for some time, and to have this validated meant a great deal to him. This very important meeting was a catalyst in relieving much of the religious pressure to stay married, and he decided to leave. What would it have been like had the priest never called him in, or if his grandmother had never given him permission to divorce his wife? He would have stayed and perhaps have been harmed or killed at the hands of his abusive wife. This is a serious situation that cannot be minimized or ignored.

Clearly, faith plays a role in why men stay in abusive marriages. When faith is used as a means to intimidate or control someone, it is misused and misguided. It is honorable to have faith and to value family, but not at the cost of abuse. From any faith or religion, I would encourage placing a high value on one's mental and physical health, and to make decisions that are in line with a self-protecting viewpoint. There are some great resources on intimate partner abuse and religion available online and in the resource section of this book.

Finances

The cost of divorce and the stress of splitting marital assets can be overwhelming. It is no wonder many men stay in a damaging relationship because their finances are a huge concern. It becomes a very daunting task to think about the change in lifestyle that comes with divorce. One man I spoke to said his wife would receive so much in child support he would be unable to sustain any kind of normal lifestyle. He said she was very abusive verbally and would go into the safe while he was at work and steal whatever she wanted. When she was confronted, she would say that they were a couple and she had a right to any and all of the assets. She would go on shopping sprees and spend thousands of dollars they did not have to spend. One time, she went out and bought a car using money from the safe for the deposit. She was not working, and had not consulted him prior to this large purchase she was making. She did not care what he thought or wanted because it was all about what she wanted. One man, after he told his abusive wife he was divorcing her, had her steal his credit card and go to Costa Rica. She spent $2,500 on the trip with another man she had just met. I would highly recommend getting financial counsel before one makes the choice to move forward with separation or divorce.

Love

"But I love her." I have heard these words spoken by many men who have declared their love for their abusive female. The powerful emotion of love and the desire to overcome all obstacles is not new to men. They feel they can conquer all, and that the love they have for these women will somehow make the way for change. Love is a very encompassing emotion and can lead people to view situations from a distorted perspective. It is like the friends who warn the man over and over again about the girl he is dating, only to have him plow right ahead and marry her to his eventual disappointment and dismay when he realizes she is an abuser.

At this juncture, I would like to say, "Slow down, think, and listen to those who know you best and know her best. What do her friends and family think? I recommend talking to someone who has a successful relationship themselves. Acknowledge to yourself you are not thinking entirely rational due to the mere fact you are in love or lust.

It is important to give yourself the permission to look at other perspectives. Are there concerns you need to acknowledge? It may be with great appreciation that you will recognize and acknowledge you have found the woman of your dreams, or you may with the same appreciation realize there are some red flags. All relationships will have issues, you must choose the issues you are willing to accept and deal with.

If you meet her friends and family and they are giving you information that concerns you then just take your time. Ask yourself if there is any validity in what is being said or if you are being overly critical. You may find that there is not and you are with a great woman. If things progress and there are no warning signs, then you may have the woman of your dreams. There is no perfect relationship, and you will have to decide what issues you are willing to work with.

If you have a great woman with a few idiosyncrasies, then give her the benefit of the doubt and work through them. If they are things that can be worked through, then work through them together.

Some of the men I have worked with have told me that they have thought that if they can just be the man that she wants, everything will be fine and she will not be abusive to them anymore. They want to make the women in their lives happy, and believe they have the capacity to change the woman's bad behavior. One of the men I interviewed, Steve, went to a therapist for a year without telling his wife because he thought if he learned how to communicate better, she would stop verbally assaulting him and hitting him. He thought he provoked her because she constantly said it was he who made her angry and made her hit him and abuse him. He thought if he could communicate better, maybe she would not get so frustrated and call him all the horrible names she used on a daily basis. He said the therapy helped him with his communication skills, but it also helped him see how abusive his wife really was. No matter what he did, she was still hostile and violent.

If an abusive woman wants to get help and wants to change her behavior, then she can, but it is up to her. There is absolutely nothing a man can do to change an abusive woman's behavior, besides leave. She will then have to get help, or move to the next victim she will abuse.

After the therapy, Steve recalled that the main thing he regretted about his relationship was taking the blame for so much of the abuse, and for staying as long as he did with a woman who had no intention of ever stopping her abuse.

Hope for Change

The belief that change is possible is a human characteristic and a strong belief. Change is possible, and I have seen many women and men change their bad behavior. However, there is a huge caveat to that statement that reads like this: "Change is possible, when both people in a relationship want the change." It is not possible when an individual does not have any insight into his or her behavior or the impact it has on others. Change is not possible if the person is manipulative, coercive, and unwilling or unable to acknowledge her own behavior. The bottom line about change and one's ability to change is that it is crucial to look at the person's *actions*, not their *words*. Make sure they are taking steps to get counseling, attending anger management groups, and doing whatever it takes. Many times, people end up with false hope in their partner only to see the person continue in the same pattern. I have seen many couples in which one of the partners has been abusive, and it is only a matter of actions and time that shows the real results of whether one has had the ability to change or not. Some people, due to their lack of insight, are not capable of change, and will make promises to change and never deliver. The proof is in the results. If there is nothing being done to change, then it is time to move on with one's life and begin a real life in a healthy relationship.

I do not know how many times I have talked to abusive women or men and they say, "he or she made me do it; it wasn't my fault." They literally believe their abusive behavior is fully justifiable and makes sense. "If he would not have provoked me, I wouldn't have had to hit him. He kept arguing with me and I just couldn't take it anymore. I couldn't hurt him anyway; he is six feet tall!" Where is the admitting of choice in this statement? Where is the personal responsibility? It is not present because there is no insight. In my anger management and batterers treatment groups, I spend a great deal of time on personal responsibility, because I want people to recognize and acknowledge that they alone are responsible for their behavior. People may be provoked and put under extreme stress with all their buttons pushed, but they are still responsible for how they respond. Once they get this, they can truly have some freedom and control of themselves without the notion someone made them act a certain way. I have spoken to women in groups who have said they felt relieved to finally acknowledge they were responsible for the abuse against their partners. It was a relief for them to face this and a starting point for real change. I have seen male and female abusers change their behavior and keep their relationships, or go into new ones with a healthy perspective. When I talk about change, I do not mean the endless cycle of abuse and apology. To distinguish between real change and this cycle, I would ask, "Do they show that they are willing to do what it takes in their *actions*? Will the person in your life see a therapist, take a class, and do whatever it takes to change her behavior? If she is not willing, then you are merely on the treadmill that will continue to take you nowhere. You must decide to get off the treadmill and break the cycle.

If your plan is to stay in the relationship, then make sure she has a plan to change her bad behavior... and find the support you will need to hold her accountable!

It is also important to analyze yourself and what your beliefs are about marriage, as well as where you will draw the line in a relationship. What are you willing to put up with? Be clear with yourself about this, because it will help you in your next relationship as you define what is important to you. Then, when someone crossed the line with you, you can say, "I will not allow you to go there with me." It is also good to look at what you need to change about your own behavior. Change is not just about her. You have been in an abusive relationship and there are behaviors you have taken on that are not healthy. Take a look at some of the things you might do that are negative in the relationship and that might be hurting your new partner. Do you have any demeaning or abusive behavior? Do you look for ways to get in arguments because you are used to and love the drama? Do you project onto your new partner the behavior of your previous partner? Do you mistrust your new partner's motives? You must bring these into check so that your new relationship will have a chance to survive.

That may sound strange to some, but I have talked to women and men who have said they grew up with a lot of drama in their households, and it is very familiar to them. It may even seem odd when a relationship is calm and going well. People like this may actually stir things up to get the reaction and drama they have grown accustomed to. Do not mistake your new partner for your previous one and sabotage what may be a very good thing.

Timing

Many men stay long after they should because they believe it is not a good time to leave. The abusive partner may have had trauma or loss in their life. The kids may be young. There are many reasons why it may not be a good time to leave, but think about your personal safety and mental stability, as well as that of your children. Make yourself and them your highest priority. You must come to this realization: There is never a perfect time to break up a relationship. You must make the choice and follow through. You do not have to have all the answers. You just have to know you have to get out and take that first step. Maybe that will mean calling an intimate partner abuse hotline or an attorney for advice. You have to realize a large part of denial is saying it is not the right time, which is a way to back out of doing something you know will be hard to do. The more you prolong those hard decisions, the worse they can become and the abuse can become worse. Make the decision to get out and do whatever it takes to follow through.

The Blame Game

Many times the victim is told it is his fault. He comes to believe her when she says it is his fault – he is trying to become who she wants him to be. Placing the blame and also taking the blame is a common occurrence in abusive relationships. The one who is being abusive justifies the abuse by focusing on the behavior of the victim. They deflect from their own behavior and place the attention on the victim. Some things they may say include, "You got me so angry I couldn't control myself; I had to hit you." They will even "flip the script" and clearly accuse you of abusing them. Several of the men I interviewed would say that the women would hit them, and if they tried to get past her or put up their hands to block a hit, they were told they were being abusive. One man said his wife had cornered him and was punching him. He thought to himself that he could easily knock her across the room, but he knew he would get in trouble. When he went to get around her and he touched her to get by, she said, "Ouch you hit me." Abusers become masters at flipping the script and many victims will begin to believe it is their fault.

For Matthew, he felt responsible for his abusive wife's behavior. He truly believed for a long time that he was somehow at fault for not helping her, despite his constant pleas for her to get help and counseling. Jeff also experienced guilt because of his wife's behavior. He joined a church because his wife wanted to go to church and he thought it would be good for his family. He spent a year studying all he needed to about faith. He tried so hard to fix the various issues and to include the spiritual things he learned. These things were very admirable and positive. Yet while he did all of this, she continued to abuse and demean him ruthlessly. She never once thanked him for anything he did, but instead criticized him. His attempts were met with physical and emotional abuse, and eventually he left.

Fear of failure

Countless men who are very ambitious and successful in their professional lives have told me they were afraid of failure. They were able to secure a great job and provide a nice home, so why could they not make the marriage succeed? They had always been able to set goals and succeed. They did not want to accept failure at any cost. They felt it was a personal reflection on them. They believed there was something they could do to make it better. They told themselves, "If I had just tried hard enough or if I had just done whatever it took to make her better." It took Mike ten years to realize that it was not going to work, and that she was not going to change. For Mike, it meant the long drive to the attorney's office to file papers for divorce. It was one of the hardest things he ever did. That is why he went back numerous times. The desire to stick to something and make it work was a driving force for him. Once he became realistic, he got out.

Getting out can be smart, and should not be seen as failure, but each person must figure out what he must do for himself. What is it that will provide him emotional and physical safety? If the answer is to get out, then he should do just that.

If an abuser continues to blame you and deny her behavior, then you are fighting an uphill battle. If she has any insight, then I would recommend counseling, where she can be held accountable for her behavior, and counseling for you to get the healthy perspective you will need to make the right choices. You will need to have good boundaries if you stay with an abuser.

Problems with Abandonment

It is a natural human emotion to fear abandonment of another human being who has been an important part of your life for a period of time. Even when most of the memories are bad, there is still a strong inclination to stay and avoid abandonment. There are many emotions that come with the loss of a relationship: sadness, loneliness, loss of hope, disappointment, rejection, and feelings of failure. For some, the idea of closing a chapter is too overwhelming and daunting. The toll an abusive relationship takes on one's self-esteem can leave one feeling unable to move forward, and physically exhausted. People my fear they will never have a healthy relationship and that no one will ever want to be with them. They have to relearn what a healthy relationship looks like and what it does not look like. For many, it is learning new relationship skills for the first time. However, there is hope. There is hope for abandoning the fear and experiencing all that life has to offer for you specifically. There will be a time when you can look back and say, "I learned a lot and I will never make that mistake again, yet I will learn to love again in a healthy new way."

Many men fear they will end up in another abusive relationship. Steve said, "How do I know the next one isn't also going to be abusive. I didn't see the abuse with my first one until it was into the marriage. She was so nice at first." Even though there are warning signs with any potential abuser, some men miss these signs and they are afraid they will make this same error again.

Jeff felt so bad about himself after he got out of his marriage that he did not feel he knew who he was or what he wanted. He had denied himself that for so long during the course of his ten-year

145

marriage. When he began new relationships, if there was a disagreement, he would shut down. He had triggers that reminded him of his past relationship. He eventually grew more comfortable and realized his new relationship was not what he had experienced in the past, and he was greatly relieved and hopeful for his future.

CHAPTER 12
Decision Time

Abusive relationships often involve an intense amount of emotional confusion. One's hope can become complicated by the crisis at hand, turning into a destructive cycle that keeps the victim in a state of paralysis and indecision. This paralysis, caused by conflicting messages from the abusive woman, may cause a man to create a false hope that things may improve. After all, there are most likely periods in the relationship in which all seems to be well. One needs to remember: crazy isn't crazy all the time. Even the seriously mentally ill at times have moments of sanity and apparent normalcy.

Characteristics of Abusive Women

Abusive women usually fluctuate between one of the following:

- From angry entitlement to total deniability
- From blaming him to half-hearted admissions
- From apathy to promises of change

The bottom line is she is all talk and no action. This leaves a man to struggle with the difference between what she says and what she does. He spends much time hoping she will do right and hold to her word but nothing ever changes for any length of time. Even when she promises to work on things, she doesn't follow through with any real effort, and the man is left with empty promise and wishful thinking.

Why So Angry?

Abusive women tend to have a sense of entitlement for their anger. One reason they lash out in such extreme ways is because they truly feel justified in their actions.

Example: Matthew

With Matthew, his wife felt entitled to wake him up in the middle of the night by punching him in the face because she was uncontrollably upset that he did not want to buy the house she wanted. She felt entitled to what she wanted, and he was impeding her desire to achieve that. As a result, he ultimately received the full brunt of her anger via her fists to his face in the middle of the night.

Denial

Many abusive women go from absolute justification to complete denial. Often times, she will mysteriously act as though the abuse never happened. This leaves a man to wonder, "Did I lose my mind last night or did she?"

When she does address it, sometimes she will only give a half-hearted apology with no real remorse. This is simply to bury the incident and quickly move on as though it wasn't an issue. This leaves the man feeling brushed off and confused. He feels empty and at a loss for resolution. Needless to say, nothing is resolved or even truly acknowledged in this scenario.

How Can You Be Sure?

Women who are sincerely ready for change will begin with a sincere apology. The question becomes: is the apology rooted in any real effort toward change? Sincerely regretting abusive behavior is a real beginning, but it is just that—a place to begin. It is certainly not the end of the problem. Abusive behavior is fueled by deeper issues within a person which must be dealt with, or the abuse will continue to happen.

When wondering if the relationship can be healed, a man should look to his partner for good intentions with positive and consistent action toward change. She may not be perfect in her efforts or have all the answers right away. But as long as there is real effort followed by action there may be hope.

10 Signals to Watch For

Here are 10 positive signals that may indicate that a domestic dispute may be reparable:

1. Genuine regret
2. Acknowledging the problem
3. Humility
4. Taking responsibility for her behavior
5. Openness to change
6. A willingness to seek professional help
7. A desire to look inward
8. Adopting a new perspective
9. An openness to work together on relationship.
10. Practicing new ways of relating

How to Fix This

The most effective way to change an abusive relationship is to find an experienced professional to provide guidance, clarity, and direction. Objectivity is difficult to find on our own when we truly care for someone. A qualified therapist can assess the situation impartially, provide sound reasoning, and

offer practical advice to rebuild the relationship. Tools and skills provided in therapy should include:
- Healthy boundaries
- Expectations
- Healthy Communication
- Using Time-Outs and other techniques
- Managing Stress
- Taking Personal Responsibility
- Insight into managing feelings

Because the societal view is biased against the truth about abusive women, it is important to find a therapist who is experienced in the area of intimate partner abuse and the capacity for *both* genders to be abusive. For more information on how to interview a therapist, refer to chapter 15 of the book.

It is important that both people attend sessions together to have both sides of the issues openly discussed. That way, differing opinions, inconsistencies, and untruths can be confronted directly. If individual sessions are needed for one or both people to deal with personal issues, it is very beneficial to pursue this *in addition to* joint sessions whenever possible.

What If It Doesn't Work?

If a woman refuses to go into therapy, a man should pursue it on his own, regardless of her decision. At the very least, he can gain some clarity for himself and assistance in dealing with the abusive relationship on his end. This will also communicate how serious he is about changing things with or without her, because, realistically, if she will not become a part of the solution, that solution will fall squarely on the shoulders of the man.

Separation

Separation is not always the first step in the divorce process. Separation can be an appropriate choice for a man who needs a break from a volatile partner. Taking time on your own has a way of clarifying things. Some find they are relieved to be apart; given some space, they may realize they do not want reconciliation. Others may realize how much they miss their partner and that working things out is what they really want.

Of course, it takes two people making a real commitment to work things out. But sadly, this will not always be the case. However, if a separation does not lead to a strong joint effort, the safety and security of separate living quarters would already be in place.

Protect Yourself

For men who are routinely being abused by the women they live with, separation can become a very important option to consider. When the risks of harm are high and there is no sign of her willingness to change, separation can be a critical move for the man.

It is not uncommon for the need for a safe separation to arise suddenly and without much notice. Therefore, setting up a back-up plan for separation is a smart thing to do beforehand on the chance that it becomes necessary.

It Isn't Easy

When leaving her is the only thing left to do, all efforts have failed, and there is nothing to suggest that any additional effort will succeed. Accepting this may be difficult. Grief in all of its stages will likely be a part of this kind of decision.

However, the pain of such a decision is not necessarily a sign that the decision itself is wrong; this is an important realization to make in order to avoid an unhealthy move toward reconciliation.

Physically speaking, pain is a signal that something is wrong—this is something to avoid. However, with emotions, this is not always the case. Sometimes there is emotional pain associated with healthy decisions. It is something to be coped with during a time of grief and growth.

Therapy is an important resource during this time, to help with the experience of grief and loss and to help resolve the experience of being abused. Support groups are another important option, which will inevitably become more available to men as the issue of women abusing men becomes more widely acknowledged.

Leaving Is OK

As difficult as it can be, there are several good reasons for a man to leave an abusive relationship with a woman:

- High-risk circumstances
- No hope for change
- To avoid any further damage, emotionally and physically
- To protect children from exposure to abuse

Conclusion

If you leave, take time for yourself and your loved ones. Once you leave spend time reconnecting with your true self and the things you enjoy. It is important to get healthy in your body, mind and spirit so seek activities that will help you do just that.

CHAPTER 13
Handling the Finances

Do you have control over the finances you share with the abuser in your life? If not, the time is now to regain access to those accounts and ensure financial stability during this tumultuous period.

Financial Abuse

Financial abuse can be difficult to manage once it begins. It is important to safeguard your credit rating and to avoid being held responsible for her actions. Many men have told me that once they discussed leaving, their partner went on exorbitant spending sprees, getting them further into debt.

Steps to Protect Yourself

A man who has joint accounts with an abusive woman should be prepared to make a few necessary changes, including the establishment of a private account. Here are some important first steps to avoid falling victim to financial abuse:

1.   Make a list of all shared accounts, leases, loans, and financial obligations. Any bills you have

should be listed so you can determine how to handle them.

2.   Call the banks and get password information so you can review the activity on each account.

3.   Create online access to all of your accounts, and keep the login information in a safe place. Online access is a great resource available on most any type of account, including credit cards, utilities, and so on.

4.   Make copies of or list the following:

- Invoices/bills
- Account numbers
- Customer service phone numbers
- Payment due dates
- Online passwords
- Wills
- Monthly recurring bills such as utilities, etc.
- Life insurance policies
- Trust documents

5.   Access via the internet or contact customer service to gather information on current passwords, how to reset passwords, and how take your name off these accounts in the event this becomes necessary.

• If you are the primary account holder, find out what your options are to remove her from the account. Typically this means closing the account, which prevents further charges from being made. This protects you from vindictive spending or any attempts to transfer balances from her single credit account onto your joint account, making you liable for her balance as well as your own.

• If you are going to remain at the residence, all joint utilities need to be stopped and restarted exclusively in your name. If you are leaving the residence, all utilities with your name listed on them should be shut down by you and re-started by her in her name. This prevents her from failing to pay the bills and making you liable to pay the charges.

6.   Make sure you have copies of any keys to property owned by you as well as keys to jointly owned vehicles, storage units, and safety deposit boxes.

7. Have your computer checked by someone experienced with computers to make sure you do not have spyware and other programs that can be put on computers to keep track of what you are doing.

8. Have your cell phone account separate from hers. The cell phone is something that can be

accessed for numbers called. You should consider having your own phone account if you are planning to leave the relationship.

9. Make sure your car doesn't have gps on it as tracking devices can be put on cars to keep track of where someone is at all times. Both men and women use this as a means to track their partner.

Handling a Quick Break

In a crisis, when separation happens rapidly, be prepared to quickly change online passwords on joint savings, checking, and credit card accounts until you can close them. Take the amount of money that is rightfully yours and transfer it into a private account using online access (this can be done 24 hours a day by computer). If this is not possible, close the account immediately. Often times, joint accounts must be closed and re-opened to remove someone from the account, so have your plan ready.

Be the Bigger Person

It is important during this time to not operate out of fear and become vindictive in your attempts to protect yourself. Your focus should be on separating safely and protecting what is rightfully yours. Spitefully leaving her penniless with no electricity is not the goal.

Focus instead on healthy boundaries and doing the right thing, despite how badly she has behaved toward you. Make sure your actions are not guided by whether she deserves to be treated well. Let your actions be guided by who you are; by the kind of man you want to be; by your goal to be a better man with a better life. If you end above reproach, you can move forward knowing you have done the right things and handled the crisis in the best way possible.

Many people call it karma or "one reaps what they sow." Regardless of your perspective or beliefs, if you do the right thing, protect yourself, and get out with a clean conscience, you will be able to move forward in a good frame of mind. Your behavior should always be above criticism, not only out of respect for the man you are, but to protect yourself against allegations of abuse.

Proceed in a Considerate Manner

If she has a right to half or some of the money in a banking account, leave that amount in the account for her. If transferring funds online is not an option, close the account immediately and put the appropriate amount of money into a cashier's check for her. Make a copy of the check for yourself to prove that you have done this, and ask the bank manager if they will hold it there for her. If not, then have the check delivered to her. Either way, avoid handing it to her in person.

Arrange the stop dates for utilities a few days in advance to allow her time to restart the accounts in her name. Notify her of these dates via email or another way that allows you a safe distance and documentation.

Allow a certain number of days for her to purchase or transfer a vehicle into her name. Make the arrangements in a documented format, and provide the instructions along with a deadline for her to follow through. Check to make sure joint vehicle payments are being made on time, and prepare to surrender the vehicle if an appropriate arrangement cannot be made between you.

Conclusion

These are methods to safeguard your financial stability. It is very important that you gather this information, store it in a safe place, and be prepared to follow through on changes quickly. It is also very important to *take these steps yourself.* Do not count on her to close accounts and make these arrangements, as this only creates another opportunity for her to take advantage. Create a plan of action, prioritizing what must come first by considering how much you have to lose. And don't wait until it's too late.

CHAPTER 14

History of Events

When a man is being abused by a woman, it is important to acknowledge that he is enduring this in a world that, for the most part, does not believe his problem exists. Many people think men are only ever the aggressors in abusive relationships. Because of this, male victims of IPA must be prepared to show proof.

The Reality of the Situation

Men suffering from abuse must be able to prove what has happened for one very important reason: *they can be arrested as "the abuser" simply because of hearsay.* When an abusive woman has a policeman standing in front of her and suddenly needs to justify her behavior to avoid being arrested, claiming self-defense can be a very tempting—and effective—strategy. I have heard many stories from men who left the scene in handcuffs after their abusive partner lied to the police. I have had men in class who have hidden in bathrooms to avoid being abused and ultimately arrested after they were attacked. It was fortunate for a few who had cell phones and were able to tape and video the incidents.

Abusive women know this well. Some have told me in group that they have used the police as a means to gain control of a situation, whether to stay in the home or to keep the children when facing divorce. They were confident they could call the police and easily have a man arrested by making a false claim.

The bottom line is: even if he is the one bleeding, she may attempt to explain it away with a claim of self-defense. Blaming the victim by claiming to be a victim is always an option for an abusive woman. Gathering real evidence to the contrary is vital.

Third Party Intervention

Oftentimes, neither party wants the police involved, but they show up at the request of neighbors or relatives. Many clients I have seen in group were there because a relative, neighbor, doctor, or teacher stepped in to try and protect the children by calling the police or Children's Protective Services. Children in the home may also on occasion dial 911 when an argument becomes dangerous. Either way, the result is the same, and an innocent man may find himself at risk for arrest.

How to Protect Yourself

Men who are experiencing IPA and want to keep accurate records should implement the following actions:

* Gather and save everything that exhibits her abuse.

* Save all communication, such as voice mails, emails, text messages, and letters.

* Collect things she has destroyed, such as clothing and any other personal belongings or property.

* Photograph evidence of vandalism before it is repaired, and keep receipts for any work done to restore damaged property.

* Get copies of any resulting medical reports.

* Always take photos of every injury and if it changes day by day, take pictures throughout the changes. Sometimes wounds present a day or two after an attack.

* If she threatens you with false allegations and extortion, recordings of these threats will provide evidence should you need to defend yourself.

* Video-capture the abuse via cell phone or digital camera.

* Make voice recordings with a cell phone or tape recorder.

* Keep cell phones locked through the keypad so information kept there is safe from being found or deleted.

* Have as many conversations as you can via email or some other documented form.

* Be sure to download all information gathered in cell phones onto a safe computer in case the phone ends up destroyed and have a third party there during conversations, especially if it is determined you are separating.

* If someone has observed her abuse, get a statement of the incident. Details can be forgotten soon after an event, so get them on paper as soon as you can.

* Have witnesses focus on facts, not opinions: what they heard her say, what they saw her do, comments others have made about what they have witnessed, and so on. If they have seen prior injuries you have sustained, or witnessed damage to belongings, they can put this in writing as well.

- Document dates, events, and outings in which these things occurred, with as many direct quotes as possible.

Conclusion

Finally, remember that abusers will manipulate, lie, and do things to get out of the consequences, so you must prepare a thorough account of what has taken place. You could end up being falsely accused if you are not cautious and careful to document what you have experienced accurately. Expect the unexpected and just be prepared.

CHAPTER 15

Help in Your Area

If you have read the pages of this book and know you are a victim of intimate partner abuse then I would like to encourage you to access these resources. The resources listed below are just some of those that are available for you. I cannot attest to the quality of the services except for my own that I am personally involved with. However, these resources are well known for their assistance to men dealing with IPA.

It is important to get help and there are many IPA agencies that provide counseling and groups. Some agencies provide assistance with the paperwork for restraining orders, as well as advocates who will attend court hearings with you.

Therapy services offer a more in depth look into how a person has arrived in the position they are in. When someone experiences abuse at the hands of a loved one it can be difficult to deal with alone. However, some time spent with an objective, experienced therapist will help you to heal and move forward with your life.

Male IPV is becoming more recognized but you will still need to search for the right therapist for you. There are great therapists that do understand the issue and can provide guidance and counseling for you and your children. If you choose one you don't feel comfortable with after a couple sessions, you can find someone else. It is important to find someone who you feel comfortable with and has an understanding of your experience through their ability to listen reflectively.

The following questions can be asked of a potential therapist to help to see if they are a right fit for you and your particular issues:

1) What is your background in dealing with clients who have issues with intimate partner abuse?
2) What is your philosophy regarding IPA?
3) What is your view on men as victims of abuse?
4) What is your view regarding one's ability to change if they have been a perpetrator of IPA?

This is good place to start when selecting a therapist to help you on your journey.

The following are hotlines and websites that provide services to men who have experienced IPA:

National Domestic Violence Hotline: 1-800-799-SAFE (7233)

The Domestic Abuse Helpline for Men and Women or DAHMW has intervention and support services for male victims and a 24 hour hotline. They also have web based resources including a 12 week virtual support group for men experiencing domestic violence.

http://www.dahmw.org

DAHMW 1888-7Helpline (743-5754)

The men's web is a resource that has extensive information for men on many issues including domestic violence

http://www.mensweb.org

The battered men website is a resource specifically for men who have experienced domestic violence.

http://www.batteredmen.com

The National Family Violence Legislative Resource Center offers many resources and updates regarding legislation and current events and research.

http://www.nfvlrc.org

A resource that empowers youth to end the domestic violence cycle.

CHAPTER 16
Final Thoughts

You are not meant to go through something like this alone. For men who have kept their abuse a secret from everyone, it is time to let someone know what you are going through. Choose a person or people you can trust to keep this private, to be discreet and supportive, and tell them what is going on. If things do not change, you may need some friends to provide a safe place to go and some assistance while you are getting things in order. Don't be afraid to reach out. Please remember there are those out there that care and do understand your situation. If you can find a local support group, join one and begin to talk to other men who have experienced similar circumstances. There is healing that can come from a group experience.

Therapists, medical doctors and medical personnel are "mandated reporters" for abuse between spouses or partners, which means they must report physical abuse to the authorities. Therefore, they can also be important for men who need to take legal measures to stop physical abuse. I wish you the courage to reach out and to see for yourself a place of peace and freedom from abuse. May your road ahead be over flowing with love from those who deserve your love.

References

Archer, J. (2000) Sex differences in aggression between heterosexual partners: A meta-analysis review. Psychological Bulletin, 126(5), 651-680.

Brown, G.A. (2004). Gender as a factor in the response of the law-enforcement, system to violence against partners. Sexuality and Culture, 8(3-4), 3-139.

Caetano, R., Vaeth, P.A.C., Ramisetty-Mikler, S. (2008). Intimate partner violence victims and perpetrators characteristics among couples in the United States. Journal of Family Violence, 23(6), 507-518.

DeKeseredy, W.S. & Schwartz, M.D. (2003). Backlash and whiplash: a critique of Canada's General social Science Survey on Victimization. Online Journal of Justice Studies, 1(1).

Desmarais, S.L., Reeves, K.A., Nicholls, T.L., Telford, R.P., & fiebert, M.S. (2012). Prevalence of physical violence in intimate relationships, Part 1: Rates of male and female victimization. Partner Abuse, 3(2), 170-198.

Dutton, D.G. (2005). The domestic abuse paradigm in child custody assessments. Journal of Child Custody, 3(1), 28-30.-The conflict of theory and data. Aggression and violent behavior,10(6), 680-714.

Dutton, D.G., Hamel, J., & Aaronson, J. (2010). The gender paradigm in family court processes: Rebalancing the scales of justice from biased social science. Journal of Child Custody, 7(1), 1-31.

Gelles, R.J., & Straus, M.A. (1988) Intimate Violence: The causes and consequences of abuse in the American family. New York: Touchstone.

Murphy, C. & Eckhardt C. (2005) Treating the Abusive Partner: An Individualized Cognitive-Behavioral Approach.

Bowen, E. (2009) Domestic Violence Treatment for Abusive Women.

Felson, Richard B. (2008) Violence and Gender Re-examined

Straus, M.A. (2006) Dominance and Symmetry in partner violence by male and female university students in 32 nations. Unpublished manuscript, Durham, NH.

Straus, M.A. (2004). Women's violence toward men is a serious social problem. In D.R. Loseke, R.J. Gelles, & M.M. Cavanaugh (Ed.), Current controversies on family violence (2nd ed., pp.55-77). Thousand Oaks, Ca.: Sage.

Tjaden, P., & Thoennes, N. (2000). Extent, nature, and consequences of intimate partner violence: Findings from the National Violence against Women Survey.

Walker, L.E. (2000) The battered woman syndrome (2nd ed.) New York, Springer.

Yilo, K.A. (2005) Through a feminist lens: Gender, diversity, and violence: Extending the Feminist Framework. In D.R. Loseke, R.J. Gelles & M. M. Cavanaugh (Eds.) Current controversies on family violence (2nd ed., pp. 19-34). Thousand Oaks, Ca: Sage.

Stith, Rosen K. Middleton, K.A. (2004). The intergenerational transmission of spouse abuse: a meta-analysis. Journal of Marriage and Family. Vol. 62, Issue 3, pp 640-654, August (2000)

Made in the USA
Las Vegas, NV
16 January 2022

41556133R10098